W9-DEK-188

THE CHORAL CHALLENGE

THE CHORAL CHALLENGE
PRACTICAL PATHS TO SOLVING PROBLEMS

MICHAEL KEMP

GIA Publications, Inc.
Chicago

GIA Publications, Inc.
7404 South Mason Avenue
Chicago, IL 60638
www.giamusic.com

G-6776
© 2009 GIA Publications, Inc.
All rights reserved.

Printed in the United States of America
ISBN: 978-1-57999-703-8

To my parents,

Drs. John and Helen Kemp,
whose love of music and
willingness to give of themselves
for the good of others has inspired so many,

and to all the singing Kemps:

Todd, Brad, Erin, and Janice
Guy and Julia Kemp Rothfuss and their family
John and Mary Kemp and their family
Peggy Kemp and David Henry and their family
Jim and Kathy Kemp Ridl
Marggi Vangeli
Jacqueline Pierce

CONTENTS

PART III
MOTIVATING FOR SUCCESS

FOREWORD

The Choral Challenge: Practical Paths to Solving Problems by Michael Kemp is indeed a welcome resource for choral music educators. Key to this monograph is the author's positive and realistic recommendations to dealing with a wide variety of issues that vocal music educators face whether working in the school, church, or community choral setting. This book has been written in response to the myriad issues Michael has faced in his many years as a conductor and clinician working with singers and instrumentalists ranging in age from elementary school through senior citizens.

Impressive is the breadth and depth of the topics included in this book. Part 1 delves into the vocal challenges that music educators face on a daily basis. Understanding that so many of the issues faced by choral singers are related to vocal technique, Michael wisely focuses attention on this issue at the beginning of the monograph. He clearly understands the complex nature of the singing voice. His pedagogical strategies clearly employ healthy and artistic singing techniques in all aspects of the teaching. He begins his monograph by identifying nearly a hundred common vocal problems, for which he offers a brief yet practical suggestion to address each of these issues. Indeed, this cumulative list covers so many of the pervasive issues that often face vocal music educators of all ages. His recommended approaches to solving these vocal issues, as well as his other suggestions in the book, provide the reader with a multifaceted approach to these challenges. His teaching strategies employ a mixture of visual, oral, kinesthetic, and tactile pedagogical techniques that allow for varied learning styles among the musicians we deal with in our individual situations.

Part 2 of the book shifts the focus to the preparation of the conductor. Michael looks pragmatically at the criteria in the selection of choral repertoire and offers useful perspectives in the conductor's study of the score. Then he segues to sixty-two functional warm-up exercises that address many of the vocal issues he identified in part 1.

He offers his insights into the area of the intentional seating of singers to gain maximum ensemble strength and tonal uniformity. This portion of the text explores issues often encountered in rehearsal but seldom addressed in any depth in many other conducting books. His realistic rehearsal psychology provides fresh insights into so many basic frustrations faced by conductors with a common-sense approach to resolving them. Of special note is chapter 15, which focuses on working with instruments. Michael's strong training as a string player brings incredibly wise insight to effectively working with instrumental forces.

As valuable as I believe the first two parts of the book to be, I find even more distinctive the topics Michael explores in parts 3 and 4. It is not an easy thing to identify and articulate effective means of motivating individuals and not sound like a "slick" salesperson. Yet, I think Michael does an impressive and ethical job of confronting issues that successful music educators must face in terms of our individual personality traits, organizational skills, artistic strengths, and challenges as we seek to become inspiring artist-teachers to our singers. He is absolutely correct that we must first be properly motivated ourselves if we are going to have any success in motivating others. He centers on such issues as the conductor's self-discipline, self-image, and care for one's own emotional and physical health, and he offers as well suggestions for keeping fresh in order to avoid the stresses that can cause fatigue and burnout in this work. He also advocates devising new, creative paradigms that will enliven our rehearsals in an excitingly productive way. He calls for greater empathy in caring for the entire singer, or to quote Michael's beloved mother and great source of inspiration, Helen Kemp: "Body, mind, spirit, voice—it takes the whole person to sing and rejoice."

In the final segment of the book Michael advocates something he has long modeled in his work. If indeed the rehearsal setting provides the singer an inviting, creative, productive, and transforming musical experience, the essential ingredients to ensure success are at hand. However, this also calls for the vocal music educator to believe fervently in his or her vocational calling and be an "evangelist" in galvanizing others to share in this mission of the choral art that transforms those who perform as well as those who will experience this great music. Consequently, whether recruiting singers for the ensemble or supporters to enable the work of the chorus, there has to be a shared vision for artistic excellence that does more than entertain.

The Choral Challenge: Practical Paths to Solving Problems will be a welcome resource in my own work as well as in my classes on conducting, child and adolescent vocal pedagogy at St. Olaf College, and the various workshops I lead annually for school music educators, church musicians, and conductors working with singers of all ages. This book witnesses to the creative ingenuity and personal sense of calling that Michael Kemp has brought to his career as teacher, conductor, and pastoral musician. He was blessed to have as role models and mentors his wonderful parents, Dr. Helen Kemp and the late Dr. John S. C. Kemp. In them he clearly had the exemplars of the pastoral artist-teachers who served others through the gift of music. Helen and John Kemp dedicated their lives to bringing beauty, hope, comfort, joy, and love through the music they shared with generations of singers throughout the world. Michael continues this model of the servant-leader in his life and work. We who are lovers of the choral art are very fortunate that he has taken the time and dedication to share this vision of practical, yet realistic, optimism for dynamic musical leadership through this wonderful monograph. It has inspired me, and I commend it to all who wish to make a practical transforming difference through choral music in the lives of others.

Anton E. Armstrong, DMA
Conductor, The St. Olaf Choir
Tosdal Professor of Music, St. Olaf College
Northfield, Minnesota

PRELUDE

HOPING FOR MIRACLES?

Midsummer. Though barely recovered from last season, you know that the new choir season is just around the corner and, with it, the usual frustrations. Your adult choirs struggle with too many aging singers and too few younger singers on whom to build a healthy future. Prospective singers for your student choirs are enticed by myriad activities that compete for what little spare time they have.

Not only are there not enough singers, but those who do come seem listless, uninspired, and undisciplined, ready to suck the vitality right out of rehearsals and you. Some of your singers have vocal problems that affect the sound and enthusiasm of your choir, but you don't know how to help them; maybe you are frustrated with some deficiencies in your own voice. Choir rehearsals, which should be opportunities for healing beauty, become at times tedious and lethargic, and you wish for miracles to solve all these frustrations, but miracles are hard to come by.

Sound uncomfortably familiar? Choral directors everywhere feel these concerns, and the real frustration comes from not knowing what practical steps they need to take to move toward solutions. If only there were some effective and reliable source that addressed these concerns.

I've written *The Choral Challenge: Practical Paths to Solving Problems* for that purpose. Its intention is to be an effective, easy-to-use resource of specific steps to solve specific problems. So enough with the negatives! You *can* solve most problems, even that older alto with the unnerving wobble, the nasal tenor with the laser-beam voice, and the bass who takes singing flat to new levels of consistency. I've included scholarly but accessible explanations of basic categories of concern, such as breath support, followed by descriptions of choir director questions in each category, suggestions for their resolution, related additional ideas, and sixty-two accessible functional warm-up exercises designed to teach specific skills.

Beyond addressing these vocal concerns, *The Choral Challenge* also includes steps you can take to recruit more singers and motivate them for consistent attendance and more sustained effort in rehearsals. Do you want to gain the support of your administrators, colleagues, and community? That's here too.

The heart of *The Choral Challenge* is that the solution to all these concerns starts with developing a fresh, new outlook. Unstoppable determination must become your "default" attitude, and your enthusiasm must be omnipresent if you are to build a great tradition and attitude in your choirs. Believe this. If you are willing to expend the effort, you can and will solve these problems.

So replace those hopes for a miracle with action. Fixing those debilitating vocal problems and filling your choir room with well-motivated singers is not an accident of fate but a direct result of a plan. Let's get started.

PART I

SOLUTIONS TO CHORAL CONDUCTOR CONCERNS REGARDING THE VOICE

INTRODUCTION: THE HUMAN VOICE

The human voice is a marvelous instrument that is effectuated by a remarkable anatomical and physiological mechanism involving breathing, laryngeal muscular function (vocal folds, sometimes erroneously referred to as vocal cords), and overarching cerebral control. Of particular interest to singers and choral conductors is the quality of the resulting vocal function, characteristics that issue both from natural ability and developed ability. It is this process of developing vocal ability that is both accessible and pertinent to choral conductors and voice teachers. The challenge is to develop in their singers the various aspects of vocal technique that have not come naturally but would add to the overall beauty and effectiveness of their voices. Hence, the natural flow of choral teaching is, first, the identification of vocal problems and, second, the application of specific solutions. Many expert physicians, choral clinicians, and voice teachers have advanced medical and pedagogical solutions to certain vocal problems, but choral conductors must prepare themselves to deal with an amalgamation of *all* the vocal problems common among choral singers. Part 1 of *The Choral Challenge* offers accessible explanations of these vocal concerns, followed by practical steps toward solutions for each.

Each of the following categories of vocal concerns lists specific vocal questions from choral conductors related directly to that concern. These questions were submitted to me by choir directors from throughout the United States and Canada during thirty-five years of teaching choral workshops. Directors in these workshops were asked to describe vocal problems they had encountered in their choir members or in their own voices that they had not been able to solve or did not fully understand. They were to describe these vocal concerns in any way that made sense to them, much in the style of public radio's *Car Talk*.

HOW TO USE THIS INFORMATION

The intention of this portion of *The Choral Challenge* is to enable a director dealing with a vocal concern to find clear, concise, accessible explanations of what causes the problem and what steps singers should take toward correcting the problem. To use this book effectively:

1. Look through "Troubleshooting Common Vocal Problems" on the following pages to locate the description of the vocal concern resembling the one you want to research. The left-hand column called "key word" will prove useful in locating your specific concern. The second column contains related questions about vocal production.

2. Read the quick answer provided in the third column.

3. Look in the fourth column to find the primary category of vocal concern related to your problem, along with its page number in the fifth column. Locate and read the overview to that primary category of vocal concern.

4. In the sixth column are secondary concern categories related to the question, with page numbers in column seven. Solving a problem often requires a combination of steps in several areas, so it is beneficial to read the overviews to these secondary categories as well.

RELATED CHORAL AND VOCAL EXERCISES

Later in part 2 of *The Choral Challenge*, there are sixty-two functional vocal and choral exercises, many of which are directly related to the vocal concerns approached in this section of the book. Each of the exercises designates the skill it is designed to improve or the concern it helps solve. Each exercise includes not only the musical notation and choral text but also instructions for how to use the exercise. These exercises can be used as additional resources in solving vocal concerns, whether in rehearsals or in individual voice lessons. So the final step is to choose exercises in part 2 that might be useful in solving your concern.

TROUBLESHOOTING COMMON

KEY WORD	VOCAL QUESTION	QUICK ANSWER
agility	naturally legato voices that have trouble singing staccato	use a brighter tone placement, more airflow, and less volume; initiations should be simple and clear, not attacked; the larynx should not be pressed too low
	voices that can't move quickly from pitch to pitch	the larynx is being held in too rigid and low a position; practice breathing in through the upper teeth and along the hard palate, and initiate singing from that position without pushing down the larynx
	teaching agility for Handel's *Messiah*	if the larynx is too low, the voice can't be flexible; when inhaling, bring the breath along the top of the mouth (hard palate) and sing from there without dropping the larynx artificially lower; then let the breath cause the voice to work...don't activate the voice by itself
alignment	bodies or heads in strange positions	start by stretching the top of your spine to the ceiling, whether standing or sitting; take an Alexander Technique lesson
blend	getting voices to blend	blend is mostly the result of vowel colors that agree; a choir that blends well generally closes the vowels slightly, meaning that all vowels are somewhat umlauted, the face embouchered (see page 69), the lips rounded, the upper lip slightly raised, and the lips are active, not placid; a blended sound is more important in some styles of music than in others, e.g., music of the Renaissance
	blending men's and women's voices	in their respective middle registers where they sing the most, men need higher, more forward placement and hence slightly more open vowels; women need a lower, more sternum-centered support and hence more focused, closed vowels; when warming up, it works well to sing the same notes but with women on /u/ (as in "soon") and men on /ɑ/ (as in "father")

VOCAL PROBLEMS

PRIMARY CATEGORY	PAGE	SECONDARY CATEGORY	PAGE
loosening the articulators	47	posture and alignment breath support and airflow	51 61
loosening the articulators	47	posture and alignment breath support and airflow tone placement and registers	51 61 69
tone placement and registers	69	posture and alignment	51
posture and alignment	51	loosening the articulators	47
vowels and consonants	75	loosening the articulators open throat	47 57
vowels and consonants	75	tone placement and registers	69

KEY WORD	VOCAL QUESTION	QUICK ANSWER
breath	singing longer without a breath	through improved breath support, use more air rather than less; with more air, the air is used more efficiently, and it lasts longer; energize consonants; emboucher (see page 69) the face to focus vowels
	not taking in enough air during inhalation	better posture and spinal alignment result in better breath support; when not enough air can be taken in, the thorax (chest area) becomes collapsed or the belly is mistakenly being held stiff during inhalation rather than letting the abdomen relax completely and the belly fill with air
breathiness	breathiness, especially in younger girls	use more air rather than trying to control it; the vocal apparatus will be able to use the air more efficiently, the air will last longer between breaths, and the tone quality will lose its breathiness
chest	developing chest tone	check alignment; work from long-distance speaking, as opposed to speaking on a phone; emboucher (see page 69) the face and raise the soft palate; have a sense of using less air on low pitches; use five-note descending scales (G_4 to C_4) moving from *mezzo-piano* on /u/ (as in "soon") to *mezzo-forte* on /ɑ/ (as in "father")
chesty	correcting "chesty" loud singing in younger voices	make sure the music is not too low in pitch (most of the music should stay above F_4, because it is easy to slip into loud, chesty sounds below that); go for vitality without loudness; use more focused vowels for warming up, and slightly umlaut all vowels, modifying the lips toward the shape for /u/ (as in "soon"); the first sound in each phrase should always be softer and then grow from there; sing sustenuto rather than note-to-note accenting; for young singers, the lower the pitch, the lighter the accent

PRIMARY CATEGORY	PAGE	SECONDARY CATEGORY	PAGE
breath support and airflow	61	posture and alignment vowels and consonants	51 75
breath support and airflow	61	posture and alignment	51
breath support and airflow	61	vowels and consonants	75
tone placement and registers	69	posture and alignment breath support and airflow	51 61
breath support and airflow	61	vowels and consonants	75

KEY WORD	VOCAL QUESTION	QUICK ANSWER
consonants	grinding r's	r's are actually not all bad; they were used as warm-ups by Roger Wagner in preparing Renaissance music...but with a more open jaw; simply open mouth and emboucher (see page 69) the face to achieve a forward placed, rich, colorful sound
	indistinct consonants	using good breath support to provide ample and consistent airflow is the key to consonant clarity; the airflow must push right into the consonants, without backing off when approaching the next vowel; the stoppages of the vocal articulators must be strong enough to create strong resistance, and the breakthrough of the air must be sudden and distinct; embouchering the face and lips adds to the distinctness
dark	throaty, swallowed sound with a slow vibrato	the larynx is jammed down too far, so breathe through the upper teeth along the hard palate and initiate sound from there, without lowering the larynx any more than it is
	overly dark, throaty, heavy voices; swallowed sound	check spinal alignment; raise the soft palate to increase the ring; when inhaling to sing, bring the breath along the top of the mouth (hard palate) and sing from there without dropping the larynx artificially lower
	overly dark vowel sounds	use the reverse vowel-color arm gauge, going from overly covered to more open vowel sounds, and then back just a bit to a good balance; also try "singing above the paper" image (chapter 5) to brighten the tone placement
dryness	dryness in the throat	drink much more water; cut back on caffeine products

PRIMARY CATEGORY	PAGE	SECONDARY CATEGORY	PAGE
vowels and consonants	75	open throat	57
vowels and consonants	75	breath support and airflow	61
breath support and airflow	61	posture and alignment open throat vibrato	51 57 81
tone placement and registers	69	posture and alignment vowels and consonants	51 75
vowels and consonants	75	loosening the articulators tone placement and registers	47 69
loosening the articulators	47	open throat	57

KEY WORD	VOCAL QUESTION	QUICK ANSWER
dynamics	voices that cannot change dynamics gradually	airflow needs to be ample regardless of dynamic levels; *piano*s take the same amount of air as *forte*s, but we tend to use much less on *piano*s, making our voices unstable; keep your placement the same on changes of dynamics, not letting the soft palate drop as you diminuendo
falsetto	when to use and how to produce falsetto	the male voice falsetto is approached with the forward placement described for women's high register, placed at the back of the hard palate, with a sensation of resonating behind the eyeballs (sometimes described as "up and over" singing); it is vital to keep the placement high and forward with the nasal passages open, or hoarseness could result; produced this way, falsetto is a safe means of marking, taking pressure off the voice in taxing high passages, especially in rehearsals; when used, falsetto should be a full, brilliant sound with forward placement
fatigue	voices that fatigue easily	the voice fatigues quickly when it is working too hard on its own; better posture and alignment open the door to better breath support and therefore to getting the air moving, letting it bring the vocal folds together; the voice shouldn't work on its own
flat	flatness of pitch	flatness usually means the tone placement is not high enough and the larynx is positioned too low; emboucher (see page 69) the face and aim the sound through the upper teeth, instead of lower in the throat; there needs to be more space in the vocal tract (check alignment), which usually means raising the soft palate in combination with better breath support and airflow

PRIMARY CATEGORY	PAGE	SECONDARY CATEGORY	PAGE
breath support and airflow	61	tone placement and registers	69
tone placement and registers	69	breath support and airflow	61
posture and alignment	51	breath support and airflow	61
tone placement and registers	69	breath support and airflow	61
		posture and alignment	51

KEY WORD	VOCAL QUESTION	QUICK ANSWER
flat	flattening as the pitch ascends	read chapter on tone placement to find described the varying sensations of placement in the lower, middle, and upper vocal regis-ters; when moving up from the lower range to the middle range, the sensations of place-ment change from the extreme front of the mouth to the dome of the hard palate (right above the tongue); when moving from middle to high range, the placement moves to the back of the hard palate, as if right behind the eyeballs; along with this attention to tone placement, make sure the airflow stays ample as you ascend, and that you do not let the soft palate drop; an embouchered (see page 69) face will also help keep the sound bright and, therefore, on pitch
	older altos who sing flat on A_4 and above	older singers are no different from any other singers who need to be reminded of good vocal habits, e.g., support and place-ment; flatting is the result of placement that is not forward; emboucher (see page 69) the face and aim the sound through the upper teeth instead of lower in the throat; there needs to be more space in the vocal tract (check alignment), which usually means raising the soft palate in combination with better breath support and airflow; at A_4 the vocal sound needs to become hooty and echoey, as opposed to the brightness of chest tone; close vowels slightly, e.g., modify /ɑ/ (as in "father") toward /ɔ/ (as in "saw")
	shrill voices that sing a quarter step flat	shrill means not enough space in the vocal tract; see chapters "Open Throat" and "Tone Placement"; once there is more space, better breath support, and therefore more airflow, the pitch adjusts (when the voice is free, it is easier to sing on pitch than off); add to the effect by embouchering (see page 69) the face and closing vowel sounds slightly by using a smaller mouth opening

PRIMARY CATEGORY	PAGE	SECONDARY CATEGORY	PAGE
tone placement and registers	69	open throat	57
		breath support and airflow	61
tone placement and registers	69	posture and alignment	51
		vowels and consonants	75
tone placement and registers	69	open throat	57
		breath support and airflow	61
		vowels and consonants	75

KEY WORD	VOCAL QUESTION	QUICK ANSWER
flat	women who sing flat above C_5 with a tight jaw	singing flat is more about tone placement than hearing inaccurately; see suggestions for "singing above the paper" (chapter 5); regarding the tight jaw, see chapter "Loosening Up the Articulators"; regarding the alignment issues, stretch the spine toward the ceiling with the top of the back of the head pulled straight up as if on a string; take an Alexander Technique lesson
hoarse	conductors who get hoarse often	be more aware of the way you use your speaking voice and the way you model in rehearsals (e.g., the way you quickly throw in correct notes without regard for your own vocal quality); take time to breathe when speaking or singing; avoid bending your head down to read your music and singing from that misalignment; always stretch the top of your spine up to the ceiling; take conscious time to breathe, and let your airflow do the work instead of your larynx
	singers who get hoarse often	most hoarseness and vocal fatigue comes from the larynx working too hard; let the airflow do the work and the larynx be incidental; keep stretching the top of the spine upwards, giving the voice more space; never sing louder than 90% capacity
	speaking voices that get hoarse easily	many good singers do not use the good habits of vocal health when speaking, e.g., posture and alignment, breath support and airflow, tone placement; project your speaking voice with airflow and support, note your posture, and let your vocal articulators be active; above all, take time to breathe when you speak

PRIMARY CATEGORY	PAGE	SECONDARY CATEGORY	PAGE
tone placement and registers	69	loosening the articulators	47
		posture and alignment	51
posture and alignment	51	breath support and airflow	61
		tone placement and registers	69
breath support and airflow	61	posture and alignment	51
		tone placement and registers	69
breath support and airflow	61	open throat	57
		tone placement and registers	69

KEY WORD	VOCAL QUESTION	QUICK ANSWER
hoarse	what to do about hoarseness	drink more water throughout the day; gargle four times a day: in a cup of hot water from the tap, mix in a rounded teaspoon of salt and another of baking soda, and gargle first with airflow but no voice, and then gargle again adding the voice on a quiet /i/ (as is "see"); avoid singing if possible; if not, mark (half sing) as much as possible, and check posture and alignment, stretching the top of the spine up; check for ample airflow; work quietly for more ring in your tone placement, e.g., chanting "nyuhm-nyuhm-nyuhm"; on the day of an important performance, warm-up with this procedure: divide the time between waking up and the performance in half; then divide the second half in half again; then again, etc., up to the performance; for five minutes at the beginning of the first segment, warm up gently (see chapters 4 and 5) at a *piano* dynamic, limiting range to a comfortable fifth ($E\flat$ to $B\flat$); then no vocal sound until the second segment; then the same process again, each time increasing range and dynamics until just before the performance, by which time you are singing with normal range and dynamics
	women who lose their voices and make a high screech like a balloon for a split second	the larynx is working too hard; get the airflow moving and let the voice work incidentally with it; then check for better tone placement, which should enable the voice to move naturally between registers; if the problem persists, see an otolaryngologist
initiations	excess breath on initial sounds	this is called aspirating the entrance; emboucher (see page 69) your face and then breathe in as if through your upper teeth, with the breath moving along the hard palate; then initiate the sound as if from that position without pushing the larynx lower; the voice should start working at the same instant that the air moves through the vocal folds

PRIMARY CATEGORY	PAGE	SECONDARY CATEGORY	PAGE
breath support and airflow	61	posture and alignment tone placement and registers	51 69
breath support and airflow	61	open throat tone placement and registers	57 69
breath support and airflow	61	tone placement and registers	69

KEY WORD	VOCAL QUESTION	QUICK ANSWER
initiations	harsh, glottal initiations	the larynx is initiating sound before the air starts flowing; the air should not only be first, but it should draw the vocal folds together, instead of the larynx working on its own
	initial-note scooper	the breath support is initiating late, just after the voice begins; work from short but gentle *mezzo-piano* staccatos that start right on pitch; then sing "My Country, 'Tis of Thee" in the same gentle staccato style, and then in a portato style (initiations like a staccato with smooth follow-through); until habitual, the singer needs to adopt this style for all singing
legato	naturally staccato voices that have trouble singing legato	in legato singing, one must be more aware of steady breath support over the entire phrase, including the consonants; correcting alignment helps
loft	loud voices that cannot sing quietly, especially in the upper register	this singer may not be in the correct voice part; check his or her comfortable *mezzo-forte* high and low notes, and then sing the first phrase of "My Country, 'Tis of Thee" in several keys to determine the most comfortable (F is baritone or first alto; C is bass or second alto; B♭ is soprano or tenor); the placement may also need more ring
	singing at quieter dynamic levels	all dynamic levels require the same amount of air, but we tend to use (produce) less when we try to sing quieter; as a result, the voice doesn't work as well; retain good alignment, and then keep good support down low while keeping the throat open and the air flowing freely

PRIMARY CATEGORY	PAGE	SECONDARY CATEGORY	PAGE
breath support and airflow	61	tone placement and registers	69
breath support and airflow	61	tone placement and registers	69
breath support and airflow	61	tone placement and registers	69
breath support and airflow	61	tone placement and registers	69
breath support and airflow	61	posture and alignment tone placement and registers	51 69

KEY WORD	VOCAL QUESTION	QUICK ANSWER
loft	developing head tone	use upwards portamento (gliding) "whoops"; then do the same with last note held (use *oo* vowel) with ample airflow; imitate old-fashioned "bah-oo—gah" horn, letting the middle high syllable go well into head-tone range, carrying the energy and airflow through to the lower last syllable
	young singers with no loft in their voices	begin with building more space in the vocal tract through better alignment and a higher soft palate; then get the air moving through blowing and sighing, speaking, and then singing; use closed vowels, e.g., /u/ (as in "soon") and an embouchered (see page 69) face for warming up
nasal	"tin can" sound	nasality issue; use reverse vowel-color arm gauge; sing "dee-dee-dee" emphasizing the consonant (*d* not *n*)
	country-western voices that don't blend	nasality issue; use reverse vowel-color arm gauge (from spread to focused vowel sounds) with smaller mouth opening; sing "dee-dee-dee" emphasizing the consonant (*d* not *n*)
	overly nasal voices	try "singing *below* the paper" (without closing off the nasal passages; chapter 5); stronger breath support will add depth to the sound; place hands over the sternum and aim the singing sound through the hands
phlegm	continual clearing of throats	drink more water, long before rehearsal if possible, as well as during rehearsals, to keep phlegm from sticking to the vocal folds; if problem persists, see an otolaryngologist about the possibility of acid reflux

PRIMARY CATEGORY	PAGE	SECONDARY CATEGORY	PAGE
tone placement and registers	69	breath support and airflow	61
tone placement and registers	69	posture and alignment open throat tone placement and registers	51 57 69
tone placement and registers	69	open throat vowels and consonants	57 75
tone placement and registers	69	posture and alignment vowels and consonants	51 75
tone placement and registers	69	open throat breath support and airflow	57 61
open throat	57	posture and alignment breath support and airflow	51 61

KEY WORD	VOCAL QUESTION	QUICK ANSWER
pitch	"helium balloon" singers (wandering high pitch)	better breath support, even for young singers, provides a physical connection that helps to focus pitch; exercise on ascending "whoops" on closed vowels, e.g., /u/ (as in "soon"), which feel centered in the sternum; also try having the singer put hands on the sternum and aim their sound through the hands
	boys singing down an octave (subsinging)	compare speaking on the phone with long-distance speech (projecting your voice a long distance); use that feeling when singing; put a fist on the chest, other hand over it, and aim the sound into the hands; use upward portamentos (slides) with good placement; then again, sustaining the final higher pitch
projection	quiet voices that cannot sing louder	the first step is to use breath support to get more air going flowing the voice; the term *louder* also involves the ability to project the voice, which comes from better tone placement; for younger girls, work through focused (closed) vowels, e.g., /u/ (as in "soon")
	helping voices project	need to develop "ring" in the voice; emboucher (see page 69) the face, flaring the nostrils, and chant "mnyuhm-mnyuhm" with a buzzy quality; then hum on a mid-range G pitch with that same buzzy quality; then the same on *ng*; then *ngaw*; then *aw*, retaining the buzz; sing a five-note descending scale (G to C) with an embouchered *v* into the upper teeth

PRIMARY CATEGORY	PAGE	SECONDARY CATEGORY	PAGE
breath support and airflow	61	posture and alignment vowels and consonants	51 75
breath support and airflow	61	posture and alignment tone placement and registers	51 69
breath support and airflow	61	posture and alignment tone placement and registers	51 69
tone placement and registers	69	breath support and airflow	61

KEY WORD	VOCAL QUESTION	QUICK ANSWER
range	limited range of only two or three notes	this usually means a lack of physical vitality; get the breath moving, and then add the voice with sighs and ascending "whoops" from the sternum; work from long-distance speech and closed-vowel sirens with the same sound; on the *forte* sirens, feel the extra power at the top; then siren up again, but sustain the high pitch; then sing the high pitch without the slide; try hands on the sternum as in the suggestions above for "projection: quiet voices that cannot sing louder"
	boys who can't sing higher pitches	work from long-distance speech…make the movements of throwing a ball while you throw the sound; use strong, low breath support (appoggio); have a sensation of using more air on upper notes; make sure that you are well aligned; sing not just to but *through* the high notes, like hitting through the ball in various sports
	range extension downwards	lower notes only project when they are bright, which means using as far forward a placement as possible; the sensation should be right in the front of the mouth; use less air on low notes; the most common mistake is to inflate the sound of low notes, meaning that they become very airy with no carrying power; low notes must retain a "ringing" sound
	range extension upwards	high notes still need forward placement, but the sensation is at the back of the hard palate, as if just below the eyeballs; the sensation is described as "up and over" sound; the soft palate stays high and the face embouchered (see page 69); have a sensation of using much more air on upper notes; relax and let the air handle it; make sure that you are well aligned, not leaning forward (keep your heels pressed into the floor); sing through the highest notes in a phrase, carrying momentum to the next note after the highest pitch, or to the silence after the final note

PRIMARY CATEGORY	PAGE	SECONDARY CATEGORY	PAGE
breath support and airflow	61	posture and alignment tone placement and registers	51 69
tone placement and registers	69	posture and alignment breath support and airflow	51 69
tone placement and registers	69	posture and alignment	51
tone placement and registers	69	posture and alignment breath support and airflow	51 61

KEY WORD	VOCAL QUESTION	QUICK ANSWER
range	tenors who can't sing high without going into falsetto	see "range: range extension upwards"; if the problem persists, check to make sure that the person is singing the correct voice part: check comfortable *mezzo-forte* high pitch and low pitch; sing the first phrase of "My Country, 'Tis of Thee" in various keys; F is baritone; the higher B♭ is tenor; the lower C is bass
raspy	raspy tone quality; rough, gravelly tone quality	use the breath support exercises provided to get the breath moving; then add the voice without initiating the effort from the larynx
	voices that sound like they are gargling	there is too little space in the throat; check alignment and raise the soft palate; this might also be caused by phlegm sticking to the vocal folds, so drink more water (long before singing and during rehearsals) to help the phlegm slide off the vocal folds; if the problem persists, see an otolaryngologist to check for acid reflux
registers	tenors who can sing high notes loudly but not at quieter dynamic levels	some singers mistakenly force loud high notes without using forward placement; their larynxes are usually jammed down, and they muscle over the top; there is little control or flexibility, and the sound is generally unpleasant; the key is to work on forward placement, aiming the sound into the upper parts of the mouth; a forward-placed, brighter sound undergirded with adequate airflow has the capacity for various dynamic levels; the airflow must remain the same for *forte* and *piano*; the tendency is for the airflow to diminish in *piano* sections, which closes the vocal tract; if the problem persists, check to make sure that the person is singing the correct voice part (see chapter 9)

PRIMARY CATEGORY	PAGE	SECONDARY CATEGORY	PAGE
tone placement and registers	69	breath support and airflow	61
open throat	57	breath support and airflow	61
tone placement and registers	69	loosening the articulators posture and alignment open throat	47 51 57
tone placement and registers	69	breath support and airflow	61

KEY WORD	VOCAL QUESTION	QUICK ANSWER
registers	women tenors who say tenor is too high for them	check alignment and open throat; then follow suggestions for a higher, more forward placement; use better breath support to produce more airflow; exercise with closed-vowel ascending glide "whoops" and "yippees" with plenty of air
	difficulty in moving between the vocal registers	use the correct placement indicated for each register, and when approaching the next register, begin changing the placement early; don't initiate sound from the larynx, but rely on the airflow; proper alignment lets the voice work more naturally
	tightening as the pitch ascends	better tone placement and airflow help the transitions as you sing higher; avoid leaning forward as the notes ascend, which causes restrictions in the airflow; stretch your spine toward the ceiling and keep your support low
	voices that crack when moving from the lower to the higher notes	there is some adjustment in tone placement necessary when moving from low to higher notes; the sensation of placement for lower notes is at the front of the mouth; then for mid-range notes, in the dome of the hard palate right above the tongue; then for high notes, at the back of the hard palate, as if just below the eyeballs; all of these placements are forward, aiming the sound into the upper area of the mouth; singers who crack (usually when ascending) are not using forward placement enough, and probably are not using enough airflow; if the problem persists, check to make sure that the person is singing the correct voice part (see chapter 9)

PRIMARY CATEGORY	PAGE	SECONDARY CATEGORY	PAGE
tone placement and registers	69	open throat breath support and airflow vowels and consonants	57 61 75
tone placement and registers	69	posture and alignment breath support and airflow	51 61
tone placement and registers	69	posture and alignment breath support and airflow	51 61
tone placement and registers	69	breath support and airflow	61

KEY WORD	VOCAL QUESTION	QUICK ANSWER
registers	vowel modification on higher pitches	when the placement is correct for the upper register and the breath support is ample, the vowels should take care of themselves without being artificially modified; it is the placement that needs modifications when going from one register to another
	women with significant breaks between head tone and chest tone	note the changes of tone placement sensations between the lower and middle vocal ranges; in approaching the next register, begin changing the placement early; practice this skill using a descending five-note scale (G to C) changing gradually from /u/ (as in "soon") to /ɔ/ (as in "saw"), and beginning *piano* and going to *mezzo-forte*; have a sense of using more air on higher pitches and less air on low pitches
ring	developing "ring" in voices	emboucher (see page 69) the face, flaring the nostrils, and chant "mnyuhm-mnyuhm" with a buzzy quality; then hum on a mid-range G pitch with that same buzzy quality; then the same on *ng*; then *ngaw*; then *aw*, retaining the buzz; sing five-note descending scales, G to C, with an embouchered *v* into the upper teeth
	voices that lose the "ring" on certain vowels	on closed vowels, e.g. /i/ (as in "see"), /u/ (as in "soon"), and /o/ (as in "so"), be sure the nasal passages are open and free to resonate; also note in the chapter "Vowel Color and Diction" the correct positioning of the tongue for various vowels
	unfocused tone quality	need more of a physical connection and vitality that comes from stronger breath support; sing a *forte* "zoom—," sustaining the final *m*, and making it buzzy and strong

PRIMARY CATEGORY	PAGE	SECONDARY CATEGORY	PAGE
tone placement and registers	69	posture and alignment	51
		breath support and airflow	61
tone placement and registers	69	breath support and airflow	61
tone placement and registers	69	breath support and airflow	61
tone placement and registers	69	breath support and airflow	61
tone placement and registers	69	breath support and airflow	61
		vowels and consonants	75

KEY WORD	VOCAL QUESTION	QUICK ANSWER
shallow	shallow, thin voices	not enough air is being used; develop the breathing cycle and then get more space in the throat by raising the soft palate; check alignment; increase vitality by using physical movements while warming up
	women with a high, thin sound	start with more space (posture, alignment, open throat), and then get the air moving through better breath support; add an embouchered (see page 69) face and raised soft palate
sharp	sharp singing	begin by loosening up physically; breathe and support intentionally lower (cup hands low in front of you with arms extended in front of the body, feeling the breath initiating from that level); slide slightly up into each note from just below the pitch, enough that you know you are doing it, but not enough that others can hear it; try sternum-centered ascending "whoops"
	sharpening as the pitch ascends	keep the breath support down low to avoid pressure creeping into the larynx; think of appoggio, the "pressing down" style of support; the throat therefore stays more open and the pitch is not affected
	sharpening on the longer final notes of phrases	the support of the airflow, and therefore the amount of airflow, is diminishing as soon as the final note initiates; the support and musical momentum must carry through the final note into the silence; avoid physically leaning forward on the final note, which constricts the airflow
	singers who change pitch when crescendoing	as the crescendo begins, the larynx is gradually being pushed too low, the ring in the placement is disappearing, and the airflow is being constricted, all of which is affecting pitch; think lower support (appoggio); avoid physically leaning forward during the crescendo, which adds to the constriction; stretch the top of the spine upwards

PRIMARY CATEGORY	PAGE	SECONDARY CATEGORY	PAGE
breath support and airflow	61	posture and alignment tone placement and registers	51 69
breath support and airflow	61	posture and alignment open throat tone placement and registers	51 57 69
breath support and airflow	61	posture and alignment open throat	51 57
breath support and airflow	61	open throat vowels and consonants	57 75
breath support and airflow	61	open throat	57
breath support and airflow	61	posture and alignment	51

KEY WORD	VOCAL QUESTION	QUICK ANSWER
shrill	piercing voices	this comes from holding the vocal tract tensely, and is sometimes mistaken as impressive power; working through the exercises provided in the chapter "Breath Support and Airflow," focus on initiating quiet sounds without effort from the larynx; what we generally refer to as power is really projection, and that comes from tone placement, not a tight throat
	brassy, brittle sound	the larynx is working too hard...let the airflow work and the voice relax; create more space with an open throat; sing sustained phrases instead of note to note
	hard, driven vocal sound	first loosen up the torso and articulators; then get the air flowing to avoid any sense of grabbing by the larynx...let the voice add incidentally to the airflow
	voices that tighten as they ascend and screech on top	keep air moving through and past the highest note in the phrase; "leave your throat out of it," but leave your nasal passages open for resonance while moving through the vocal registers
sticking out	older women's voices that stick out	"older" is not a problem, but some older singers do need reminders of good vocal habits, e.g., better posture and support; get the air moving, and then don't press so hard with the voice; sing beautiful phrases with smooth contours rather than note for note; let phrases begin and end a little quieter than in the middle
	squeaky sopranos who stick out on high notes	get more space by opening the throat; make the vowels more vertical by modifying them to a more closed position, e.g., /ɔ/ (as in "saw") to /O/ (as in "so")

PRIMARY CATEGORY	PAGE	SECONDARY CATEGORY	PAGE
open throat	57	loosening the articulators breath support and airflow	47 61
breath support and airflow	61	loosening the articulators posture and alignment open throat	47 51 57
breath support and airflow	61	loosening the articulators	47
breath support and airflow	61	tone placement and registers	69
breath support and airflow	61	vibrato	81
breath support and airflow	61	open throat vowels and consonants	57 75

KEY WORD	VOCAL QUESTION	QUICK ANSWER
sticking out	sticking out on *forte* passages	not enough airflow causes a swallowed (lowered larynx) sound that doesn't blend; leave the larynx alone and let the air lead; then get the placement appropriate for that register
	basses with beautiful low notes who stick out above G3	the lower notes, although sounding rich and dark, are probably too swallowed, with the larynx pressed too far down; that type of placement cannot be carried above G3; the solution is to develop a healthier mixed voice throughout; specifically, there needs to be more ring in the voice, a higher placement, and work from the larynx through better breath support and airflow
	women tenors who don't blend	since a woman tenor will be singing predominately in her chest range, she must work toward more forward placement in her vocal production by raising the soft palate; her sound will also blend better if she embouchers (see page 69) her face and closes her vowels slightly, e.g., modifying /ɑ/ (as in "father") toward /ɔ/ (as in "saw"); except for occasional emergencies, it is preferable to avoid assigning women to sing tenor on a regular basis; the inherent danger is that they will lose any sense of head tone (lighter mechanism) in their vocal production
support	older singers lacking breath support	good posture and alignment is generally possible and certainly beneficial at any age; once properly aligned, begin by blowing air, then humming and sighing to get the connected feeling of breath support

PRIMARY CATEGORY	PAGE	SECONDARY CATEGORY	PAGE
breath support and airflow	61	tone placement and registers	69
tone placement and registers	69	breath support and airflow	61
tone placement and registers	69	posture and alignment breath support and airflow vowels and consonants	51 61 75
posture and alignment	51	breath support and airflow tone placement and registers	61 69

KEY WORD	VOCAL QUESTION	QUICK ANSWER
tension	excessively tight jaw; singing almost through teeth	allow the jaw underneath to be slack, while at the same time emboucher (see page 69) the face; repeat the word "yah" over and over, letting the jaw flop; initiate singing sound on an /O/ (as in "so"), placing the edges of the hands on your cheeks between the jaws; work for the hallow openness of an open throat; allow the airflow to initiate vocal sound without activating the jaw; the singer could be forcing the voice to work instead of allowing it to be a natural byproduct of airflow
	squeezed throat with a spread sound	close vowels, e.g., /ɪ/ (as in "sit") modifying toward /i/ (as in "see"); smaller mouth shape; emboucher (see page 69) face
	strained, pressured, "in pain" sound	emboucher (see page 69) the facial muscles and use smaller mouth shape; start all phrases simpler and quieter by getting the air flowing freely first, and then adding the voice on that air; begin phrases quietly and then let the sound grow
	tense voices with no flexibility	rehearse with kinesthetic motions, e.g., swinging arms or swaying; use more air and less volume; warm up with light staccatos that have forward momentum
	tightness in the throat; visible tension in the body, neck, and face	often symptomatic of general physical tightness and a habit of making the voice work with little airflow; try combining kinesthetic movements with vocal warm-ups, e.g., swaying or swinging arms; proceed from blowing air to sigh-singing, and then to simple, slow glides down a whole step; sing these while looking in a mirror, not allowing any sign of tension; take an Alexander Technique lesson

PRIMARY CATEGORY	PAGE	SECONDARY CATEGORY	PAGE
loosening the articulators	47	open throat	57
loosening the articulators	47	open throat	57
		tone placement and registers	69
		vowels and consonants	75
loosening the articulators	47	open throat	57
		breath support and airflow	61
loosening the articulators	47	open throat	57
		breath support and airflow	61
loosening the articulators	47	posture and alignment	51
		open throat	57
		breath support and airflow	61

KEY WORD	VOCAL QUESTION	QUICK ANSWER
tension	tightness and pressure in the throat	hold your breath and feel where the closure occurs; then make that spot as open as possible; avoid grabbing initiations, but instead, start them gently, simultaneously with the airflow
vibrato	no vibrato	starting at puberty, vibrato is a natural part of the voice; although it shouldn't draw attention, it is characteristic of a mature voice, and will be a part of a voice unless there are muscular or space constrictions upon the larynx; if the breath support and resulting airflow are insufficient, the larynx engages, doing the work meant to be incidental to the upward airflow; that affects vibrato; no discernable vibrato comes from an improperly engaged larynx being in too high a position; loosen the articulators and open the throat; then relax and sing on the air; easy kinesthetic movements while warming up can also help
	slow, wide, labored vibrato	although the sound is the opposite vibrato extreme, slow, wide, or labored vibrato is also the result of restrictions around or stresses on the vocal apparatuses that disallow this natural phenomenon; the basic solutions are remarkably similar to those for no vibrato; also note that a wide, labored, or slow vibrato (generally including a swallowed tone quality) comes from an improperly engaged larynx in too low a position; check spinal alignment and head and neck positioning; when inhaling to sing, take in the breath as if along the top of the mouth (hard palate) and sing from there without pushing the larynx artificially low

PRIMARY CATEGORY	PAGE	SECONDARY CATEGORY	PAGE
open throat	57	breath support and airflow	61
vibrato	81	loosening the articulators	47
		breath support and airflow (with emphasis on support)	61
		tone placement and registers	69
vibrato	81	loosening the articulators	47
		posture and alignment	51
		breath support and airflow (with emphasis on airflow)	61
		tone placement and registers	69

KEY WORD	VOCAL QUESTION	QUICK ANSWER
vibrato	child singers with extreme vibrato	it is rare to hear a noticeable vibrato in prepubescent children; it often happens that children try to imitate popular vocal music sound, inadvertently lowering the laryngeal position; this is clearly not healthy, and not in the best interests of either the child or the choir; choir directors and voice teachers must not attempt to artificially develop vibrato in the way string players are taught vibrato; first loosen up the torso and articulators, check alignment, then make sure ample air is flowing; start with blowing air as if blowing out a candle, and work from that into vocal sighing and then sigh-singing (a combination with elements of both); work with closed vowels, e.g., /u/ (as in "soon")
vowels	spread, shallow vowel sounds	use the vowel-color arm gauge, going from spread to closed vowel sounds, and then back just a bit to a good balance; also emboucher (see page 69) the face, using a smaller mouth opening and more active lips
	indistinct or neutered vowels; all vowels sound the same	the lips need to be more active, with the jaw opened slightly wider for certain vowels; emboucher (see page 69) the face and constrict and lift the upper lip; aim the vowel sounds there, making sure the airflow is ample and the larynx is not pushed down too low
	correcting vowels that stick out, e.g., i (as in "see") and e (as in "say")	emboucher (see page 69) the face and lips; pull out upper lip and leave it there ("fish-lipping"); modify all closed vowels, /ɪ/ (as in "sit"), /ɛ/ (as in "bed"), and /e/ (as in "say") slightly toward /i/ (as in "see"), using that same /u/ (as in "soon") lip shape while leaving the nasal passages open

PRIMARY CATEGORY	PAGE	SECONDARY CATEGORY	PAGE
vibrato	81	loosening the articulators	47
		posture and alignment	51
		breath support and airflow	61
vowels and consonants	75	posture and alignment	51
		open throat	57
		tone placement and registers	69
vowels and consonants	75	tone placement and registers	69
vowels and consonants	75	tone placement and registers	69

KEY WORD	VOCAL QUESTION	QUICK ANSWER
vowels	e vowels (as in the first part of the diphthong "say") that don't blend	emboucher (see page 69) face and slightly umlaut all vowels, using a smaller mouth opening; the vowels $/I/$ (as in "sit"), $/\varepsilon/$ (as in "bed"), and $/e/$ (as in "say") all modify slightly toward $/i/$ (as in "see")
	over-enunciation; exaggerated jaw movements	work on sustained singing, with all the sounds tied together; hold the head still and move the jaw only moderately, letting the active lips do most of the work of changing the vowel sounds
	singers with clear a vowel (as in "father"), who can't produce an i (as in "see")	the tongue is too far back...probably even on the $/a/$, although it doesn't show as much as on the $/i/$; put the tip of the tongue against the lower teeth and then see the information about tongue positions for various vowels; be sure to keep the nasal passages open on $/i/$ (as in "see") and $/u/$ (as in "soon"); let the airflow do the work instead of the larynx
wispy	wispy-sounding young singers	young singers need to feel a sense of compression in their breath support, a physical connectivity and vitality more like the rest of their lives; healthy vocal shouts of "hey" and "ho" along with foot stomping and arm movements get the energy started
yawning	yawning when trying to sing	start with correcting alignment; when inhaling to sing, bring breath along the top of the mouth (hard palate) and sing from there; when the larynx is dropped too low and posture is slumped, yawning often results

PRIMARY CATEGORY	PAGE	SECONDARY CATEGORY	PAGE
vowels and consonants	75	open throat	57
vowels and consonants	75	posture and alignment	51
vowels and consonants	75	breath support and airflow	61
posture and alignment	51	breath support and airflow tone placement and registers	61 69
posture and alignment	51	open throat tone placement and registers	57 69

CHAPTER I

LOOSENING UP THE ARTICULATORS

In the same way that runners stretch their muscles before actually running, singers need to stretch their bodies; that is, they need to lubricate and build the flexibility of the various vocal articulators (face, jaw, lips, tongue) before singing warm-up exercises.

LUBRICATING THE VOICE

Several hours before a rehearsal or performance starts, drink one to two glasses of water. Drinking just before singing is moderately helpful, but drinking water earlier allows time for it to be assimilated by the body, providing lubrication for the voice. Avoid caffeine, since it has the opposite effect on the voice; it dries out the voice. Whenever possible during singing responsibilities, keep a bottle of water with you and take small sips often.

LOOSENING THE TORSO

Grab hold of the two handles of an open door (or any stable object that is about waist high). Back up about a foot and a half, and pull out with your lower back, holding that position for a count of twenty. Then, for personal warm-up, hold a broomstick or similar long handle across your shoulders behind your neck, arms draped over the handle. Keep the top of the spine in a tall position throughout. Now, initiating the movement from your sternum, turn slowly to the left, looking over your left shoulder. Then repeat on your right side. Go back and forth between the sides several more times. In choir rehearsals where broomsticks are obviously impractical, take your left arm under your right arm and hold it at the elbow. Then pull the elbow to your left, turning the entire torso and looking over your left shoulder. Repeat on the right side. Finish this loosening of the torso by rolling your shoulders forward and up in circles with elbows held slightly out from the body, hands in a conducting position—palms down, keeping your hands horizontal to the floor as if pointing forward with your little fingers. Always keep the top of the spine stretched tall. Note that rolling your shoulders back and then up (instead of the more helpful forward and then up) creates unwanted tension in the neck and displaces correct neck and spinal alignment. Proper spinal and head alignment is discussed later at length (see chapter 1).

ABDOMINAL EXERCISE

Developing better strength in the abdomen, lower back, chest, and shoulders makes a substantial difference in the vitality of conducting gestures. Consider finding out about light weight-training for the chest and shoulders, and specific exercises for the abdomen. There are many effective abdominal exercise devices that would be of significant benefit for conductors.

LOOSENING THE NECK

Standing or sitting with good posture and keeping the top of the spine tall, drop your head all the way down until it is hanging free. With the head still lowered, shake your head slowly side to side, as if saying no. Slowly roll the head back up to its normal position, always keeping the top of the spine tall. Twist the head all the way to the left as if looking over the left shoulder; then the same on your right. Now, without collapsing your spinal alignment, let your left ear lean down toward your left shoulder. From that position, let the head roll slowly forward and then up to the right side, right ear leaning toward the right shoulder; then back down and center again and back up to the normal position. Make sure your breathing is regular throughout—avoid holding your breath. Now pretend that a flashlight is coming out of the top of your head with the beam going straight up. Make little imaginary circles on the ceiling, first starting one direction, and then the other.

LOOSENING THE FACE, LIPS, AND JAW

Using the musculature of the face, brow, and head, wiggle and stretch your face all around. Now massage the temple muscles on both sides of your forehead with your finger tips, and then your whole face. With the jaw closed, purse your lips as far forward as possible into the shape formed for /u/ (as in "soon"). Then move back and forth between extreme facial changes for that $/u/$ and a very wide $/i/$ (as in "see"), activating that part of the face. Now repeat this facial exercise more rapidly. Then place your fingers lightly over the back part of your jaw (right under the ears). Clench your teeth and locate with your fingers the masseter muscles that bulge. Unclench them and gently massage that area with your finger tips. Now that the jaw is loose, do an imitation of circular open-mouthed chewing. Then, while continuing to chew, speak the following words several times each: "Yum, yum, yum" and "meow, meow, meow." Check to see that your spine is extended up toward the ceiling. The flexible movement of the articulators (face, jaw, lips, tongue) is to singing and diction as fingers are to the violinist.

TONGUE POSITION

One of the most common vocal problems is a throaty, swallowed sound, usually accompanied by a slow or wide vibrato and a tendency to flat. These vocal characteristics are caused by a tongue position that is too far back in the throat. It is, admittedly, confusing to singers that such a back-tongue position produces a sound that seems to the singer to be mature and powerful. In reality, this tongue position decreases resonance and the voice's capacity to project, causes a slowing of vibrato because the throat is not open (the vocal tract is constricted), and causes the voice to neither tune nor blend well.

SETTLING THE TONGUE FORWARD

Tongue stretches in these pre–warm-up procedures help develop healthy forward positioning of the tongue. Stretch the tongue out and down toward the chin as far as you can, making your tongue fat (like a spatula). Hold it there for five seconds. Let it slowly slide back into your mouth, but only until the tip of the tongue touches the back of the lower front teeth. Do this several times. Then, with the tongue again stretched out and down, begin speaking numbers, from one to twelve, three numbers to a breath. Relax for a moment, and then put the tongue back out, this time saying the months of the year, a few at a time. Articulate as well as you can. When the tongue returns to its normal position, the tone quality is often noticeably more free and clear. In a mirror, the pharynx (the open space behind the tongue) should be visible while singing, not hidden by an arching back of the tongue. To build flexibility in the now-forward tongue together with a loose jaw and ample airflow, whisper, "Lah-lah-lah-lah-lah-lah" several times, being sure not to collapse spinal and head alignment.

RELATED VOCAL CONCERNS AND SUGGESTIONS

- Be aware that the tongue should *always* remain a little forward, with the tip of the tongue touching the back of the lower front teeth.
- On vowels related to /ɑ/ (as in "father"), the tongue should be fat, touching both side edges and the front of the lower teeth.
- For vowels related to /i/ (as in "see"), the still-forward tongue is narrower, not touching the sides of the lower teeth, and humped toward the front (unlike the /ɑ/ vowel, for which it is humped a little farther back).

I am indebted to the writing and philosophies of Dr. Robert Sataloff, MD, DMA, Professor of Otolaryngology at Jefferson Medical University, Thomas Jefferson University in Philadelphia, and to Michelle Horman, CCC-SLP, voice pathologist and singing-voice specialist, for sharing her expertise in this area.

CHAPTER 2

POSTURE AND SPINAL ALIGNMENT

Singers strive for good posture because it allows the body to function at maximum efficiency. The process of breathing and breath support are enhanced, the air flows upward unimpeded, the vocal folds are drawn together naturally, and the vocal sound is able to take full advantage of the resonators. However, an inherent danger is that too rigid a posture is almost as detrimental to good singing as bad posture.

THE ALEXANDER TECHNIQUE

The Alexander Technique suggests that, rather than setting ourselves in a certain posture, we would be better to think in terms of balance, mobility, and integration throughout the whole body. The following introduction to the concepts of the Alexander Technique was written for *The Choral Challenge* by Judith Grodowitz, an AmSAT Certified Instructor and extraordinary teacher in New York City:

> *The Alexander Technique suggests that with an optimum organization of the body, all the movable parts will work together in dynamic connectivity. Imagine a three-dimensional model of a human skeleton. Within this model, the skeleton acts as a kind of powerful, flexible scaffolding, which is mobilized by the muscle tissue surrounding it. Muscle tissue can have a very fluid, streamlined quality when there is an egalitarian distribution of effort.*
>
> *The balance of the head in relationship to the torso is essential in this organization. Head balance influences how weight and effort will pass through the whole skeletal structure. Thus, it is vital to our ease, efficiency, and freedom. To locate the area where the head balances and moves in relationship to the spine and torso, stand looking forward with your gaze out, as if you are looking into the eyes of someone exactly your same height. Do not get "set." Now,*

gently make a small circle with the tip of your nose, as if you are writing in air with your nose. You are now moving your head at the actual joint where your head and the top of your spine meet. Notice the difference between this place and the top of a T-shirt collar. We often initiate movement of our heads from the T-shirt top area—which is much lower down than where the head and spine actually meet. By initiating movement and freedom at the top of the spine, we take pressure off of the movable parts below. We decompress. This is good news for moving and breathing.

With the Alexander Technique, when things are working well, "good posture" is really just a "happy byproduct" of what we call "good use of the self"—that is, how we function as an integrated whole in any activity. For specialized activities such as conducting and playing music, we can look to our execution of the simplest tasks—such as standing, sitting, and walking—and discern the underpinnings of how we habitually organize ourselves to "do what we do." These patterns will usually be present, and often exaggerated, in the more complex activities of our art.

Alexander Technique work brings awareness to the phenomenon of how we coordinate mind and body. We engage a process whereby we can elicit change at a very core level. We learn how to "talk with ourselves" in the moment, and, with the most delicate of thoughts, to fluidly shift to a use of the self that is beneficial and energizing. When we impose postural imperatives and alignment formulas on ourselves, we often get stiffening and positioning—the very thing that interferes with fluidity and resonance. Try to begin with sensing and rethinking/reorganizing yourself, versus "placement." This way, you can begin to shift out of habitual "misuse." We don't want to exchange one "rigid shape" for another "rigid shape." Rather, we work to exchange rigidity for mobility and support. By encouraging movable relationships between "parts" that are clearly articulated/ acknowledged, we attain dynamic support. "Balance" is the point of most possible movement. . . even in apparent stillness.

Proper Alignment for Standing

Although our aim should not be a set, rigid posture, it is true that as singers we must strive for healthier alignment. Alexander Technique lessons will help you fine-tune your own unique alignment issues, but there are some basic suggestions that will be of general benefit to us and to our choir members. Regarding standing, think of the feet as tripods. In a neutral stance, there is a three-way balance between the base of the big toe, the base of the little toe, and the center of the heel. Be aware of the strong connection between the body and the feet (including the heels), as if the heels were aimed down into the floor. This configuration below changes the alignment of the body above, placing the top of the spine more in line with the heels, rather than leaning slightly forward when placing one's weight on the toes. This balance also effects a healthy change in the latissimus muscles in the lower back and also the lower abdominal muscles, creating a gentle firmness, the opposite of a sagging feeling. The knees should not be locked back, but have the flexibility as if you were about to sit from a standing position, just forward of the locked position. When attempting to "stand straight," many of us hold our chests too high, causing some alignment problems at the top of the spine and head. To correct this tendency, think of the top of the spine, rather than the sternum, leading the posture. Aim your spine toward the ceiling, whether sitting or standing. Let the sternum and chest (thorax) relax into a natural position. We need to get away from the static idea of "holding" a certain stance and instead get into the pliant idea of "aiming" the posture into better alignment. Rather than attempt a certain stance for singing and conducting, we should continually strive to lengthen our bodies with flexibility.

PROPER ALIGNMENT FOR SITTING

Sit directly on the sitz bones, not on the fleshy muscles in front or behind. The sitz bones are the ischium bones of the pelvis, located in the center of each buttock; these are the bony parts a person feels when sitting up straight on a firm surface. These bones are like rocking chairs, so there are a variety of positions that are well seated. Placing your weight right on the sitz bones lengthens the torso and spine, puts the head in good alignment, and allows flexibility in the muscles needed for breath support. Placing your weight forward of these bones causes a swayback posture, stiffness in the shoulders, and head out of alignment. Placing your weight behind them results in a collapsed chest, inflexible breath support muscles, and head out of alignment. Many singers who slip into this posture problem also sit back in their chairs with their ribs pushing against the chair. The intercostal muscles of the ribs are interdependent, and, if any portion of them presses against a chair back, for instance, none of the set of intercostals will function efficiently. These rib cage muscles are an important part of the breath support mechanism. Without them at full strength, exhalation necessary for singing is compromised. Having choir members sit forward on the edges of their chairs guards against this problem and helps singers sustain better alignment.

RESULTS OF ALIGNMENT

Being out of alignment makes one feel compressed and saggy. Your body is working against itself. When you get into a more healthy alignment, you will feel a release from such compression into length, width, and depth. In many cases, your head will feel further back than it was, although it is now simply in more of an aligned state. Being in alignment is not meant to be a static placement but rather a positioning of the total body that allows maximum flexibility and balance, and that allows the body to function at optimal efficiency and with minimal strain. When properly balanced, the head can move freely in all directions, as if you had eyes in the back of your head, which were looking all around. In all head positions, whether looking up, down, or to either side, the top of the spine should continue to strive for lengthening, remaining tall but flexible. Rather than collapse that alignment when you look down, begin that movement with a lengthened, "tall" spine and nod your head down from that tall position.

HOW ALIGNMENT AFFECTS THE EYES

Proper spinal alignment permits a straight forward gaze, which carries with it the appearance of strength and authority. Collapsed spinal alignment necessitates an upward gaze, suggesting an unsure or servile manner.

ALIGNMENT FOR CONDUCTORS

Regarding alignment for conducting, hold your elbows slightly away from the body with the palms down. The shoulder ball-and-socket joints work better and stay healthier when the hands follow the lead of the little fingers, almost as if you were pointing at the choir with your "pinkies" while conducting. The Alexander Technique concept of feeling a better connection with the floor (aiming the feet into the floor) and letting your conducting gestures follow the little fingers makes conducting clearer, stronger, and less tiring.

A SAILOR'S ANALOGY

An analogy for this approach to the coordination of better spinal alignment is that the body works together in connectivity in the same way that sailors in the old days used to pull in the anchor ropes on ships: a sailor's left hand grabbed hold of the rope and pulled. Part of the way through that left-hand pull, his right hand grabbed hold and began pulling. Once the right hand had taken over the connection, the left hand released and reconnected further up the rope. The "connectivity" of the effort was never broken. The Alexander Technique suggests that the body's connectivity should never be broken, from the feet to the top of the spine, to the head and eyes. It must work as one entity, finding the path of greatest efficiency and least strain. Proper alignment is not about finding and memorizing one perfect position but rather about a continuous movement toward lengthening and balance.

ALIGNMENT AND BREATH SUPPORT ASSESSMENT BREAKS

Occasionally, give your singers a one-minute timeout during rehearsals to remind themselves of optimum and flexible lengthening of their alignment, and to reloosen their necks and torsos. Have your singers check themselves out to see if they are breathing well, exhaling several times to make sure their body is working as a whole, and that the abdominal area is flexible and free. This just takes a minute, gives them a little break, and helps them make adjustments toward the kind of spinal lengthening that allows efficient breath support and removes unnecessary strain from vocal production.

I am indebted to an extraordinary teacher of the Alexander Technique in New York City, Judith Grodowitz, an AmSAT Certified Instructor, for many of these insights.

CHAPTER 3:

OPEN THROAT

Having an open throat means maximizing pharyngeal space during vocal production. Vocal sound is initiated by air flowing through the vocal folds, causing the vocal folds to vibrate. This process of the folds being drawn together is called the Bernoulli effect. The elasticity of the skin pulls them back apart, and the process repeats itself at incredible speed. This is the genesis of vocal sound. This sound is then colored and magnified by resonators in the pharyngeal tract and the mouth. An open throat allows maximum space around the vocal folds for upward airflow, maximum use of the resonators in enhancing the quality of the vocal sound, and less tension on the larynx and the vocal folds within.

ALIGNMENT CHECK

The logical first step in developing a more open throat is to check and correct alignment. (See chapter 2.)

THE BIG THROAT

This image has proven helpful in experiencing what an open throat feels like. Imagine that your throat is a spacious, empty column dropping down into your body and that when you inhale in preparation for singing you can reach your hand down into that large throat and pull out some rich, echoey quality from inside your body. Your throat has to remain very open in order to get your imaginary hand in and out. This imagery helps singers open the throat and keep it open as the air moves upward during exhalation and phonation.

THE SURPRISE THROAT

Another way to experience an open throat is to imagine being suddenly surprised by something, physically resulting in a sudden, open-mouthed gasp and a lifting of the facial muscles. The same effect is felt when going outside into freezing weather when you weren't expecting it, resulting in the same open-throated, quick gasp. This is the type of open throat that singers should experience during inhalation, giving space in the vocal tract.

FINDING AND RAISING THE SOFT PALATE

Retaining this newfound open-throated feeling, add a little more resonating space in the back top of the mouth by raising your soft palate. In order to raise the soft palate, you must first know where it is. Say the word "hang—" and note the physical sensations on the final *ng*. To produce the /ŋ/ sound, the soft palate lowers and the back of the tongue raises until they touch. This pinpoints for you where the soft palate is located, it being the upper level that is touched by the tongue. In order to learn to voluntarily raise your soft palate, locate that /ŋ/ place again with the word "hang—," and then, right where you feel the back of the tongue touching the skin above it during the "ng," raise that soft-skin area—called the soft palate—thereby creating maximum vertical space. Practice this by saying, and then singing, "hang—aw—," making a sudden maximum contrast between the two positions. Embouchering one's face (see chapter 5) seems to increase the space, which we call the open throat.

OPEN-THROATED SPEECH

Retaining this open throated feeling, now say the following open vowels and diphthongs several times each: "ah—," "ay—," "ow—," and "I—." Avoid glottal shocks (harsh sudden phonation) or any sense of attacking the vowels; rather, initiate each vowel gently and continue in a sustained style, letting the sound ride on the airflow. The sound should be hooty and echoey. Don't manipulate your voice or try to project at this point (that comes in a later chapter). Let the sound go with the flow, and let your larynx find its natural position without forcing it in either direction.

OPEN-THROATED CHANTING

Still retaining this open feeling and hooty, echoey quality, lightly chant on a G pitch the following sentence, which is replete with these open vowel sounds: "My mamma's in the Bahamas." Staying aware of the constant airflow, speak this sentence as sustained as possible, lingering on the nasal consonants and using inflection. Then, without adding weight or losing the open space, sing these same words using the music in warm-up exercise number 8 in chapter 12. Concentrate on reaching down into that "big throat" (open throat with maximum space for resonance), eliciting a dark, echoey quality. Begin in E♭, moving up by half steps.

CHAPTER 4:

BREATH SUPPORT AND AIRFLOW

The term *breath support* refers to the coordinated physical process of breathing, which provides the force to send the air stream up through the body to the larynx, where it causes the vocal folds to create sound. *Support* is a term often used by choir directors and voice teachers, but one that is widely misunderstood and rarely explained well. It concerns the coordinated cycle of inhalation (taking air in) and exhalation (pushing the air up and out), which results in the upward airflow necessary to singing. It does not refer to the common misperception of holding in your stomach in the classical pose of a model and rigidly keeping it there. Proper breath support does not refer to a single posture or stance for singing but rather to a combination of physical movements that control the breathing process. Breath support is the power source that keeps the pressure off the vocal mechanism, protecting against excess muscle tension in the neck and vocal tract.

INHALATION

During inhalation, the diaphragm contracts and moves downward while the intercostal muscles of the rib cage expand, spreading the ribs. The combination of these two muscular actions creates a vacuum that pulls air into the body. In order to create the necessary space for the incoming air, the abdomen must completely relax during inhalation, resulting in a protrusion of the belly. Keeping this area rigid would limit the space for the incoming air. Less air in means less air out, and therefore less air available for efficient phonation and sustained vocal effort. Inhalation should be relaxed and quiet, breathing in through the nose when time permits. If the inhalation is noisy, either the spinal and head alignment is incorrect or the abdomen isn't releasing completely. The space needed for efficient inhalation is therefore insufficient, and the body reacts by trying to muscularly suck in air that should normally be pulled in by the vacuum of the waiting space.

EXHALATION AND PHONATION

During exhalation (the expulsion of air necessary for speech or singing), the muscles reverse their roles from the process of inhalation. The diaphragm now relaxes and the abdomen contracts, exerting upward air pressure, which pushes air out of the lungs and up through the larynx. The area at the belly button moves inward, without allowing the chest to collapse. Inside the larynx are the vocal folds, two flexible flaps of skin. When the air goes between the folds, they are drawn together by what is called the Bernoulli effect. Then the elasticity of the skin pulls them back apart, creating one vibration, and the process continues at incredible speed. These vibrations are our vocal production, the initiation of speech or singing, which we call *phonation*.

IT'S A MATTER OF BALANCE

If you needed to scratch your nose, what muscles would be involved in bending your arm to bring your hand to your face? The biceps, of course. But if only the biceps were engaged, you would slap yourself in the face. It is the triceps that function as the opposing muscles that give control to the movements of the biceps. Muscles work in this "push-pull" counterbalancing act in all physical movement. During exhalation, the primary muscle is clearly the abdomen; its counterbalance muscle, the diaphragm.

This explains the confusing discrepancy between the singing descriptions of various professional singers, some of whom describe the feeling of support as high or pulled up, while others say low or pushed down. The Italian term for breath support is *appoggio*, which means "to lean." Webster, however, defines support as "to hold up or serve as a foundation for." Whether one senses "leaning down" or "holding up" in their support process, the results must be unrestricted for ample upward airflow.

BREAKING COUNTERPRODUCTIVE NATURAL HABITS

What typically happens when a choir member is instructed to take a deep breath? More times than not, the abdomen is sucked in with chest held high and shoulders raised, with the air usually held by tightly closed vocal folds (sometimes inaccurately called cords). As we have already discussed, these natural physical reactions by the abdomen, chest, shoulders, and vocal folds are all counterproductive to singing. During inhalation, the abdomen should have disengaged direct control while the diaphragm contracted downward, allowing the belly to flop forward without constraint. The chest and shoulders should not have been impacted at all, and the vocal folds should never close tightly and hold air under pressure. Because during inhalation these counterproductive tendencies are so pervasive, the correct process for inhalation is both difficult to teach and to learn. Of the two-part cycle of breathing, it seems relatively easy to activate the abdomen in pushing the air out, but once that is done, it is quite difficult to completely relax the abdomen for the next inhalation. The assimilation of this complex cycle of inhalation and exhalation in your own singing technique is aided immeasurably by the use of good posture and spinal alignment in both the standing and sitting positions.

When breath support is achieved correctly, it provides a steady and ample airstream, which in turn results in an unwavering vocal sound. Proper breath support also protects against throat tension. Although such breath support is a natural skill at birth (note the way newborns breathe), most youth and adults have to relearn the once-natural process of correct breathing and breath support.

GETTING THE BREATH MOVING

An integral part of a singer's daily practice or a choir's warming up should be refining the skills of breath support and getting the breath moving. This involves doing the following:

1. Check posture and alignment, so that the cycle of breathing is unrestricted.

2. For inhalation, activate the diaphragm and relax the belly, creating a vacuum into which the air rushes. If time allows, breathe in through the nose.

3. Activate the abdomen and exhale through the mouth, as though blowing out a candle. Repeat three times, making sure to release completely after each exhalation, relaxing the belly for the next inhalation.

4. Repeat the exercise by exhaling slowly on a sustained *s* three times, releasing completely after each.

5. Check your head alignment to make sure that it is not falling forward and down on the exhalations. This often happens to conductors looking down at their music or to singers with bifocals.

ADDING THE VOICE TO THE BREATH

Now that we have the breath moving, we need to let the vocal folds inside the larynx work sympathetically within that airflow. We want the vocal folds to be activated *without any conscious work in the larynx*, being drawn together by the Bernoulli effect of the airflow. Although the larynx actually has the capacity to initiate vocal sound on its own, the health of the voice and the quality of the vocal sound depend upon the larynx not working on its own, but rather allowing the vocal folds to be drawn together involuntarily, the result of the upward airflow.

COMBINING AIR AND VOICED SOUNDS

Building on the above procedures, now add voice to the airflow by doing the following:

- Take several cleansing sighs—slow, breathy, quiet releases of tension. Use these cleansing sighs throughout rehearsal to break the tension and keep the air moving.

- Make two short blows, two *s*'s, and two *v*'s (through your upper teeth, with the same feeling as the *s*), releasing the abdomen completely after each.

- Make two short *s*'s and two siren *v*'s (up and down).

- Sing a series of four siren *v*'s, each one higher than the last.

- Sing two siren *v*'s, followed by a siren on the word "vain," retaining the same feeling of the *v* clear through the vowel.

EXERCISES USING THE "V" OR LIP TRILLS

Begin with descending 5–1 (scale degrees) glides with either the *v* or lip trills, starting with E♭ major (B♭ down to E♭) and moving down by half steps. If using the *v*, make sure it is placed forward and high with plenty of buzzy quality. Your mouth should not be too open and your face should be somewhat "embouchered" (more on this subject in chapter 5). *Lips trills* are made by placing the closed lips forward and slightly up, and blowing air between them, causing them to vibrate. If this is difficult, try barely pushing on the edges of the lips with our fingertips. Now sing the descending 5–1 slides again in E♭ major, this time moving up by half steps. Think mostly about the cyclical breath support and the airflow it produces, and allow the vocal sounds to be a sympathetic part of that. Remember to let the airflow do the work, not the larynx.

Using the same v or lip trills and style, try these variations:

- 5—1—5–4–3–2–1 (using E♭ major)

- 1—5—1; 1–5–8–5–1 (beginning with C major and moving up by half steps, and back down)

In this last exercise, do not aim at (stress) the highest pitch, but aim past it, bringing the top note into the musical line, keeping the airflow consistent and avoiding the tendency for the voice to hit the top note.

INITIATION OF SINGING SOUND

A clear, unobstructed opening sound is a result of timing the airflow and vocal phonation to occur at exactly the same instant. If these do not occur simultaneously, one of two problems occurs. Starting the vocal folds in motion just before the airflow begins creates a glottal stroke or shock, a harsh vocal jab that is detrimental to vocal health and destroys the smoothness of the vocal line. The opposite problem is starting the airflow just before the vocal folds are initiated, which is called aspiration, causing the initial pitch to be less accurate and the tone placement to be not as forward.

To find the balance between these two extremes, first say and then sing the words "I" and "high." The first tends toward glottal shock. The ideal balance is to be found in the word "high" when the h aspirate is not pronounced enough to be heard, but simply allows the air to open the throat at the same instant that the vowel begins. The two words should be pronounced much the same, with slightly more aspirate in "high."

Using staccato exercises can be a danger in warm-ups, in that singers may inadvertently develop a habit of making glottal stroke attacks, which are detrimental to vocal health and musicality. If you do use staccato exercises, don't allow the staccatos to be too short or harsh. Even staccatos should have a linear essence. Make the last note of staccato exercises a longer legato note, and support it into the silence. For the most part, warm-ups based on connected legato phrases are more beneficial to the voice.

OTHER IDEAS FOR DEVELOPING SUPPORT

These images, although not meant in any way to be factual, have proven to be effective means in eliciting better breath support.

- Singing should not feel as if the source of the sound is in the mouth and our job as singers is to push it out of the mouth and down. Rather, singing should feel as if the source of the sound is low in front of the body, just below the belt, as if held in our extended arms like a basketball. As singers we should feel as though we were pulling the sound in and up from there, through the head, and out the back of our heads. The resulting physical sensation is better breath support and more forward placement.

- Instruct the singer to put the fist of one hand on the sternum (thumb against the chest) and the other hand on top of that fist, pushing both into the sternum. Then have the singer sing /ɑ/ (as in "jaw") on a G pitch, aiming (centering) the sound through their fists. Correct posture and spinal alignment is important. This image is especially effective with younger boy singers whose voices have recently changed and who have never sensed the physical connection of more mature breath support.

- When working on breath support, use ascending portamento grunts (upward slides) with either hums, v's, or the vowel /ɑ/ (as in "jaw") as an effective exercise. If using /ɑ/, it is important to keep an open throat, but do not open the mouth too wide. After several of these ascending slides, releasing on the high pitch, begin the same way, but this time sustain the highest pitch, retaining the physical connectivity of the upward slide. This exercise may effectively be combined with the previous "fist on sternum" suggestion, especially for young, recently changed male voices or for anyone experiencing pitch problems.

- Singers experience more natural breath support when moving up the scale than in descending passages; therefore, they should act as if ascending in descending passages. In other words, singers must be proactive about supporting their breath in musical lines that descend in pitch.

- Some professional singers say using more air on high notes helps keep the throat open and using less air on low notes makes those pitches clearer and guards against inflation, an unfocused tone quality in which air escapes through the vocal folds.

IMPORTANT REMINDERS

- When using strong breath support, be sure that the parts of the body above the diaphragm, intercostals, and the abdomen remain flexible, unstrained, and unaffected by the strong physical support below.

- When exercising the body for general health, always keep the breath moving, exhaling steadily during major efforts. Holding your vocal folds closed tightly together during physical exertion or groaning or counting harshly out loud with exercise routines can cause vocal abuse. The rule is that during heavy exertion, you should always blow a steady stream of air. Between exertions, let your belly relax for inhalation. The timing of the breathing cycle is everything in exercise.

I am indebted to four exceptional voice teachers—Julia Kemp and Guy Rothfuss of Abington, Pennsylvania, and Margaret Baroody and Michelle Horman of Philadelphia, Pennsylvania—for their vocal expertise in this area, as well to the writings and philosophies of Dr. Robert Sataloff, Professor of Otolaryngology at Jefferson Medical University, Thomas Jefferson University in Philadelphia.

CHAPTER 5

TONE PLACEMENT AND VOCAL REGISTERS

Using the vocal skills discussed so far should result in a relaxed, open-throated, hooty vocal production, but one still lacking in clarity of tone and pitch, in resonance (projection), and in endurance. These can be developed through adjusting the singer's tone placement, the sense of where the sound is initiated.

The most common placement problem is a throaty, swallowed sound, sometimes accompanied by vibrato irregularities. This is the result of the tongue being positioned too far back in the mouth, jamming the larynx artificially low. Therefore, the placement adjustment most often needed by singers is to move toward a so-called forward tone placement, sometimes referred to as frontal or anterior resonance, and described as frontal buzz or ring. Some professional singers prefer the term "resonance on the hard palate." Their concern is that "forward placement" calls to mind a thin, squeezed sound. Their substitute term helps singers place the sound on the hard palate, resulting in a fuller, richer sound. But because "forward placement" is a common term, it will be used as this explanation continues. Here are some suggestions for developing forward tone placement.

THE SINGER'S FACE

Along with the principles of correct posture and alignment, a person's visage is integral to gaining better forward placement. I use the phrase "emboucher your face" as the first step in helping singers find frontal buzz. Embouchure normally has to do with the position of the lips in the playing of wind instruments. But the resulting sensations in the face are an asset in developing better vocal placement for a singer. Some voice teachers refer to this visage (face forming) as "flaring the nostrils." With the tips of your index fingers, touch the places toward the bottom of your nose where the nostrils and cheeks meet. Right where you feel your fingers on your cheeks, raise your cheeks (hence, flaring the nostrils). Also raise your "mustache" area (use your imagination, ladies). With your face in that position, say the diphthong /ɔɪ/ ("as in "joy") several times fast, allowing your facial muscles to be very active. Retain that feeling.

RAISING THE SOFT PALATE

Add to this facial formation the raising of your soft palate. Some directors use the image of standing the vowels up vertically in the throat. Experience the sensation of heightening your soft palate by first saying "ah" and then a small-mouthed "aw." The physical difference felt between the two in the space above the mouth is a higher soft palate on the "aw."

In striving for more forward placement, it is important to not open one's mouth too wide when inhaling. This often results in an artificially lowered larynx and a throaty, swallowed sound—the opposite of forward placement. To avoid this, imagine inhaling through your upper teeth with the air flowing along the hard palate at the top of the mouth, refraining from any special effort to lower your larynx. Then, without stopping to hold the air first, immediately sing from the same high place in the mouth. This initiates the sound with forward placement, rather than trying to get the sound forward once you are already singing.

The inhalation and the initiation of singing (phonation) should be one continuous motion. Avoid breathing in, holding the breath momentarily by closing the vocal folds tightly, and then reopening the vocal folds, which is unnecessary strain on the voice.

THE HUM-BUZZ

With the visage "embouchered" and the soft palate raised, have the singers "hum-buzz" (a buzzy-sounding hum aimed into area above the teeth rather than below) on a unison G pitch. Don't make the sound pretty; the exercise is about developing resonance and carrying power. Next, still using the unison G, sing an open-mouthed buzzy "ng" (/ŋ/). Then starting with the same buzzy "ng" (/ŋ/), sing "ngah-ngah-ngah," making sure not to lose the buzzy quality when going to the "ah" (/ɑ/) portion. Do not open the mouth too wide, which would diminish the buzz. Finally, sing "ah" by itself with that same buzzy quality. Aim the sound into your lips, just in front of your upper teeth. To feel and hear the difference, alternate singing "ah" with and without the buzzy quality. In reality, we need an appropriate balance between that extreme forward "buzzy" placement and the more beautiful lofted sound (open-throated hooty quality). The buzz makes the voice project well and clarifies pitch and diction. Loft in the voice adds color and beauty. An appropriate balance gives the singer . . . everything!

SINGING "ABOVE THE PAPER"

Another effective tool for developing better placement control is to have the singers take a piece of paper and place it between their slightly opened teeth. If a choir needs more frontal buzz in its tone quality (which most do), instruct them to mentally aim all of their sound *above* the paper (not acoustically accurate, but an effective image). Make sure they are using good spinal and head alignment, and that, when they hold the paper between their teeth, they don't thrust their heads forward.

If, on the other hand, the choir's tone quality is overly bright to begin with and lacks warmth and depth, put the music between the slightly opened teeth, but in this instance, tell them to sing *below* the paper. The resulting sound is more open-throated, deeper, and richer.

FRONTAL CONSONANTS

For more work on developing forward placement, use vocal exercises that incorporate anteriorly produced (frontal) conso-nants—i.e., *t, m, n, v, th, l, w,* and *z.* With these consonants, the initial sound begins automatically with forward placement, and the singer must be sure that the vowels following these frontal consonants remain forward in placement. Begin by chanting frontally initiated phrases such as "Wow, we won a ten!" keeping the face embouchered and the lips active (chanting is a sustained, light, echoey half-speech/half-singing). In the final word "ten," use more of an Italian "eh" ($/ɛ/$) in the top half of the mouth, so that the high placement doesn't drop at the end of the phrase. The initiating w's create not only forward placement but also beautifully colored vowel sounds.

Then sing these same words on the scale pitches 1–3–5–6–5—, beginning C♯ major, and moving up by half steps to A♭ major. Also try singing the words "me oh me oh me oh me oh me—" with ascending and descending scales (1–2–3–4–5–4–3–2–1—), again using the keys indicated above. This exercise allows a singer to sense the forward resonance throughout the phrase, carrying over the natural resonance of the m's into the o vowels.

FINE-TUNING TONE PLACEMENT

Since it is generally accepted production, it seems obvious that concentrating on forward placement is all we need to think about. As simple as that . . . or is it? The truth is that forward placement requires small adjustments according to where the pitches lie, and those adjustments are different for men and women.

Voices have natural registers or pitch groupings, each with its own characteristics and placement needs. Vocal production requires slightly differing sensations of placement as the voice moves from one register to another, much as a bicyclist shifts gears when going up or down hills. To make matters more complicated, those adjustments for men and for women in the same relative pitch levels of their voices are not the same.

REGISTER AND PLACEMENT SUMMARY

All singing should have resonance on the hard palate, forward placement. The voice should feel like a ball floating on top of a fountain or stream of air (referred to as "singing on the breath"). The sense of where that ball is floating, although always in the relative area of the hard palate, shifts slightly forward in some registers more than others. Think of the device used in shoe stores to measures the length and width of feet. If a much smaller version of that were turned upside down under the hard palate, it could move slightly forward or back in that basic area. That's what placement is doing. More volume comes from adjusting wider in this image, but the placements should always be somewhat high and forward. Allowing the placement to slip back and down results in flat singing.

The pitch ranges for each register are approximate, with the registers for lower voices being slightly lower in pitch than those listed, and those for higher voices being slightly higher. Note also that the relative register pitch ranges for women and men are slightly different.

MEN'S LOW REGISTER (F_2 UP TO E_3*)
WOMEN'S LOW "CHEST TONE" REGISTER (G_3 UP TO D_4)
> The most forward placement, with the imaginary ball floating just behind the upper teeth. Brighten the vowel color as you descend in pitch.

Pitch numbering is according to the International Acoustic Society: C_4 is middle C, C_3 an octave below middle C, C_5 an octave above middle C, etc. The pitch letters from any given C up to the B above receive the same number—e.g., F_4 is the F above C_4 (middle C).

MEN'S MIDDLE REGISTER (E_3 UP TO C_4)
WOMEN'S MIDDLE REGISTER (D_4 UP TO C_5)

Moderate forward placement, with the imaginary ball floating on the front edge of the dome of the hard palate, in the middle of the roof of the mouth. This is a slender sound, the most like speaking. The airflow is especially important in this register. Images singers use to describe singing in this register are "draw the sound out of the throat into the mouth, instead of pushing it up from below"; "start the tone from above"; "drink in the tone."

MEN'S UPPER REGISTER (C_4 UP TO A_4)
WOMEN'S UPPER REGISTER (C_5 UP TO A_5)

The least forward of the forward placement positions, with the imaginary ball floating behind the eyeballs (in the back section of the hard palate). There is a feeling that the sound is coming from high in the face. An image used by singers is thinking "up and over."

THE DIFFERENCE BETWEEN LOUDNESS AND PROJECTION

Forward or high tone placement gives the voice the ability to project. A *mezzo-forte* vocal sound with good forward placement will project further than a *forte* sound without adequate forward placement—e.g., a throaty, muffled, swallowed sound with the tongue too far back. When working to get your choirs to project a bigger sound, first unify the forward placement, and then see to it that the singers retain that forward placement at all dynamic levels. Not only will the *forte*s be powerful, but the quiet dynamics will project as well. Uniform tone placement also enhances choral blend.

THE OVERLY NASAL SINGER

Nasal singing (singing noticeably in the nose) has three strikes against it: it is an unpleasant sound, it projects that unpleasant sound strongly, and, because it has little loft (head voice), it does not blend. As unpleasant as it is to hear, nasal singing is not as difficult a vocal issue as one might assume. The nasal passages are in fact important resonators for adding color and size to the smallish sounds that initiate from the vocal folds. They add "ring" (forward placement) to our voices, which helps our voices project. To accomplish all these good things for our voices, the nasal passages need to be open and free to resonate. Therefore, in correcting the overly nasal singer, we don't want to go overboard and close off the nasal passages completely. The overly nasal singer simply has too much of a good thing and needs to add more echo, or "loft," to their natural nasal resonance in order to arrive at a more balanced tone placement.

HOW TO CORRECT OVERLY NASAL SINGING

- To correct overly nasal singing, first adjust the singer's basic posture, spinal and head alignment, and then work on developing an open throat (increasing the pharyngeal space during voice production; see the suggestions in chapter 3).

- Make sure there is ample airflow, which also helps create more space.

- Use the "paper between the teeth" image (discussed earlier in this chapter) and have the nasal singer sing *below* the paper, which usually results in a more open throat and more loft in the voice.

- Use images such as "turn up the echo feeling."

- Warm up the overly nasal voice using an umlauted *ee* vowel (see chapter 6 on vowel color) preceded by the consonant *d*, singing on a G pitch: "dee-dee-dee-dee-dee—." The typical overly nasal singer will usually sing "nee-nee-nee-nee-nee—" by mistake, because *d* and *n* are produced in the same way, except that the *n* is nasal and the *d* cannot be. Rather than correct the nasality, correct the consonant, asking that the *d* be clearer and that the singer sustain the open feeling of the *d* through the *ee* that follows.

- Try combining the above suggestion with having the singer place the fist of one hand on the sternum, covered by the other hand, and then try to place the sound into their hands. This often creates a sense of physical connection that was missing.

I am indebted to two exceptional voice teachers, Julia Kemp and Guy Rothfuss of Abington, Pennsylvania, for their vocal expertise in this area, as well to the writings and philosophies of Dr. Robert Sataloff, Professor of Otolaryngology at Jefferson Medical University, Thomas Jefferson University in Philadelphia, Pennsylvania.

CHAPTER 6

VOWEL COLOR AND DICTION

Vowels give beauty to vocal sound, while consonants clarify enunciation and add rhythmic energy. Both vowels and consonants require ample and steady airflow, and, therefore, adequate breath support. The flexibility of the articulators, the facial muscles, the cheeks, the lips, the jaw, and the tongue are also integral to clear diction.

TONE PLACEMENT VS. VOWEL COLOR

Although the two terms are often used interchangeably, *vowel color* and *tone placement* are completely different issues. Tone placement refers to the percentage of ring (buzz) and loft (echo quality) in a voice, and the singer's sense of where the sound is focused. Vowel color, on the other hand, has to do with the individual forming of the different vowels, any of which will have more ring or loft according to the natural characteristics of the individual voice. The vowel changes are not produced by the larynx. The variances in vowel color come from the shape of the lips, the width of the mouth opening, the amount that the soft palate is raised, and whether or not the nasal passages are open to resonate.

INTERNATIONAL PHONETICS ALPHABET (IPA)

It is impossible to discuss vowel color without having a way to give examples of the various vowel sounds. As we proceed, I will use the common International Phonetics Alphabet (IPA) symbols with reference words for each. Conductors and voice teachers unfamiliar with these symbols will find them a valuable resource.

BASIC RULES FOR VOWELS AND VOWEL MODIFICATIONS

1. For all vowels, the tongue should be forward in the mouth, with the tip of tongue touching the inside of the lower teeth. This position helps avoid a swallowed, throaty sound and a slow vibrato usually caused by the tongue being too far back in the throat.

2. For open vowels such as /ɑ/ (as in "father"), the still-forward tongue should be spread flat and wide on the sides (touching the teeth all the way around), and humped slightly toward the back of the mouth.

3. For closed vowels such as /i/ (as in "see") and /u/ (as in "soon"), the still-forward tongue is narrowed at the sides and humped toward the front of the mouth.

4. For uniform choral blend, all vowels should modify toward being umlauted, with the lips in the shape of a high embouchered /u/ (as in "soon"). Some directors refer to this a "fishlipping." As an example, an /i/ (as in "see") vowel should have the lip shape of /u/ (as in "soon"), the resulting sound being close to a German umlaut *ü*. When "fishlipping," it is essential to keep your nasal passages open for resonance and to "emboucher" the face.

5. Generally speaking, most singers should use a smaller mouth opening, resulting not only in more beautiful focus and blend, but also more consistent tone placement and increased ability to sing comfortably through the *passaggio*, the transition notes between the registers. Rather than dropping the lower jaw down to sing, think of lifting the upper jaw up.

6. The dark vowels—/u/ (as in "soon"), /o/ (as in "so"), /ʌ/ (as in "sung"), /ɔ/ (as in "saw"), and /ɑ/ (as in "father")—are all /ɑ/ inside the mouth, with the jaw opening slightly wider as one moves toward the more open vowels, such as /ɑ/ (as in "father"). The unique sound of each vowel comes from rounding and extending the lips. Guard against making these vowel changes with the back of the throat, dropping the soft palate. Although this is physically possible, tone placement and accurate pitch are compromised, and the "ring" (resonance) of the voice quality is lost completely on /o/ (as in "so") and /u/ (as in "soon") when the soft palate drops.

7. The bright vowels—/i/ (as in "see"), /e/ (as in "say"), /ɛ/ (as in "bed"), /æ/ (as in "sat"), and /ɪ/ (as in "sit")—are all basically /i/ (as in "see") inside the mouth, with the jaw opening slightly wider as one moves toward the more open

vowels, such as /ɪ/ (as in "sit"). For all these bright vowels, use embouchered lips with a small opening, singing as if out of the middle of the upper lip. This focuses the sound and guards against spread vowels.

8. An /ɑ/ (as in "father") vowel should generally modify toward the opening sound of /ɔɪ/ (as in "joy"), or at least to a closed-mouth /ɔ/ (as in "saw"), producing a similar effect to umlauting. As an example, "My country, 'tis of thee" would be pronounced "Moy cawntry tis awv thee."

9. For the /æ/ vowel (as in "cat"), allow the jaw to open slightly wider, adding resonance and opening the throat.

10. In the same way, to avoid the sound of a throaty, swallowed, grinding *r*, simply open the jaws slightly. In fact, an open-mouthed *r* was used as a regular warm-up of the Roger Wagner Chorale when preparing to sing Renaissance music. It produces an echoey, hooty, chantlike quality, although one must remember to retain enough open space in the throat.

VOWEL COLOR ARM GAUGE

For correcting both vowel colors and tone placement, place your right arm in front of your chest, elbow straight down and fingers straight up, with the right elbow in the palm of your left hand tucked into your ribs. With the elbow stationary, your upright arm will be moving right and left similar to the needle, or pointer, of a dial gauge. Instruct the choir to sing a G pitch on any vowel you choose. With your arm beginning on the right side, further instruct the choir to begin with a shallow, spread vowel sound. As your arm gradually moves from right to left, the choir should gradually move from an overly shallow vowel sound all the way to an overly dark, swallowed sound when the arm is on the far left. Then, without hesitating, gradually move your arm back the other way, stopping and sustaining the sound when your ears tell you the vowel is just right—not too throaty and not too shallow. Repeat the exercise with several other vowels. This exercise has the advantage of being equally effective at the same time for singers who tend to both extremes, because by its nature the exercise picks up everyone along the way and then brings them to the same balance.

THE VOWEL FORMANT SERIES

Although the above rules are generally effective for all singers, there are certain differences between men and women regarding which vowels are most natural for them in particular registers and what their placement needs are, according to the "Vowel Formant Series" (for more information, see William Vennard's *Singing: The Mechanism and the Technique* [New York: Carl Fischer, 1967]). Women usually need more loft (echoey, hooty head-tone quality) in their mid-range, while men need a brighter, more forward-placed resonance (see chapter 5 on tone placement and vocal registers). The conclusion to be drawn is that, in choral situations, it is often most effective to warm the women up on /u/ (as in "soon") and the men on /ɔ/ (as in "saw") in their mid-ranges, even using these different vowels at the same time in the same exercise (see Warm-up Exercise number 62 in chapter 12).

PROJECTING CONSONANTS

So what makes consonant sounds project? Although most singers know to sing vowels with good breath support and consistent airflow, that well-intentioned support and airflow often diminish when the vowel approaches a consonant. A consonant is a partial or complete stoppage of the airflow or the vowel sound, which is caused by a barrier—e.g., the lips, the tongue, or the soft palate—placed in the way of the air or vowel. In order for a consonant to be heard, the air (for explosive consonants) or the vowel (for voiced consonants) needs to move into those barriers with full strength and break through them, the resulting impact becoming to our ears the desired consonant sound. If the air or vowel intensity diminishes prematurely before the "big hit"—even if the lips, tongue, or soft palate go through the correct motions—the impact will not be strong enough to be heard. The airflow and vocal forward momentum cannot slow down before or after a consonant. Push the consonant into the silence if at the end of a phrase, or into the next vowel sound if in mid-phrase.

BASIC RULES FOR CONSONANTS

1. The consonants must be ahead of the beat—crisp and not drawn out—so that each pulse of music begins with a vowel. At the end of the syllable, the energy must continue past the consonant into the next vowel.

2. Consonants with pitch—*d, b, g, j, l, m, n, r, v, w, y, z*—must have the same pitch as the vowel that follows them.

3. Initial consonants must be voiced before the beat, especially the "double-bump" consonants of the English choral tradition, which combine one of the voiced consonants *b, d,*

or g with another consonant—e.g., *br*, *gr*, or *dw*. These double-bump consonants in reality constitute a separate, added syllable before the beat.

4. The voiced consonants *b*, *d*, and *g* are produced in exactly the same way as their related explosive consonants *p*, *t*, and *k*, except that voiced consonants are made with the voice activated, whereas explosive consonants are made with air only. Note that the breath support for both is the same and the airflow must be ample for both. Differentiating carefully between the two enhances the clarity of a choir's diction.

5. The nasal consonants, *m*, *n*, and *ng*, cannot be sung any louder, so in order to be heard, they must be placed slightly earlier than other consonants and sustained longer.

6. When a word or syllable ends with a consonant, it is generally elided with the beginning of the next word, in effect becoming the initial sound of the next word—e.g., "Lord is" becomes "Lor-dis." The exception is when the conductor determines that the second word ("is") should receive more dramatic emphasis, in which case "Lord is" becomes "Lor-duh-is," with the staccato "duh" occuring before the beat and a glottal separation before "is," which comes directly on the beat.

7. To practice the steady breath support needed for consonants, sing "My Country 'Tis of Thee," making an overdone, bad imitation of an Italian dialect: "Myuh_countuhryuh_tis_ofuh_theeuh, sweetuh_landuh_ofuh_liberty," and so on. Note that all the words are connected, the sound never stops, and the intensity of the vowels and airflow does not diminish when approaching a consonant. There is connectivity and sustained energy between the vowels and consonants. Now put a little bit of this technique into your normal singing.

CHAPTER 7

VIBRATO

Vocal vibrato is a fast-moving variance in pitch and intensity that adds warmth, color, and emotion to the sound. It is a sympathetic reaction to neurological impulses, which occur between five and seven times a second; therefore, this is also the frequency of vocal vibrato oscillation. Although the sound of most instruments has noticeable vibrato, instrumentalists artificially imitate what is a natural quality in the human voice in order to add similar warmth to the sound of their instruments.

TWO FUNDAMENTAL POINTS

There are two fundamental points about vibrato that are essential to its understanding by choral conductors and voice teachers.

First, vibrato cannot be artificially developed. It is not a learned skill. After puberty, vibrato gradually becomes a natural part of a well-supported and unrestricted voice. Any attempt to artificially develop vibrato—e.g., as in the way vibrato is taught to stringed instrumentalists—would without doubt be harmful to the voice.

Second, almost all cases of vibrato concerns—whether slow, wide, fast, or the absence of—are the result of unnatural pressures on or within the vocal apparatus that are affecting or disallowing this natural phenomenon. The path to overcoming vibrato problems is through finding and getting rid of any unnatural throat restrictions. We shouldn't do anything to the vibrato itself. We simply need to remove these restrictions through better vocal technique and spinal alignment, and then vibrato stands a good chance of working as intended. In many cases, this approach alone can help correct vibrato abnormalities.

WORKING WITH VIBRATO CONCERNS

Find a way to invite the singer in for an individual session. Most singers who have vibrato abnormalities are either unaware of them or are sensitive about the subject, often fearing that they will be asked to stop singing in the chorus. Directors should handle the invitation with sensitivity. If the singer has vibrato concerns, that usually also means there is vocal discomfort, or that the act of singing is not as easy as it could be. Rather than say, "Come see me so we can work on your vibrato problem," say, "I've noticed that you seem uncomfortable in some aspects of your singing voice. I think I may be able to offer some suggestions that might be helpful."

At the beginning of the lesson, have a short conversation with the singer to put him or her at ease. This is also your chance to listen to the quality of the speaking voice. Unless the speaking voice shakes uncontrollably—a sign of possibly more serious neurological or physiological concerns—you now know that there is the probability that the vibrato problem can at least be improved, if not corrected completely.

NO VIBRATO

For any vibrato abnormality, correcting the singer's spinal and head alignment is the first step. For a singer with no vibrato, the problem is often not enough airflow, which means inefficient breath support. There needs to be a better sense of physical connection with the rest of the body, a more athletic approach to singing. This lack of physical connection probably shows itself in bodily stiffness, rigidity, and a lack of energy when singing. See chapter 1 for ways to help the singer get rid of the stiffness and stimulate the body to be more vitally engaged when singing. Exercises accompanied by kinesthetic movements or quasi-dancing should also help get the body to be more involved. See chapter 4 for ways to teach better breathing and breath support habits.

WIDE OR SLOW VIBRATO

For noticeably overdone vibrato—wide, labored, or slow—the technical approach is much the same as for the singer with no vibrato. Stretch into a better spinal alignment (checking especially the position of the head), loosen up the torso and the vocal articulators, and get the air flowing with the voice. What appears so different between singers who have no vibrato or too much vibrato is the typical personality of each. Although both are too tense vocally, the no-vibrato singer is often quieter, understated, and completely under control. The too-much-vibrato singer is usually gregarious, overstated, aggressive, a born leader, pouring maximum energy into singing. But in both cases, whether physically restricted or overzealous, the body is getting in the way of the voice. There is usually tension in the posture; the torso is held with too much rigidity; the whole breathing process is compromised with not enough air getting through. That means vocal production is not as natural as it should be, and this results in vibrato problems.

The combination of better alignment, physical connectivity and flexibility, and improved breath support will result in the singer's airflow becoming ample and consistent, and soon vibrato should begin to appear.

SPEAKING ON THE AIR

Working from a non-pressed speaking voice, show the singer how to speak "on the air" with the same gentle, hooty quality as the vocal sighs, as if the voice were a surfboard incidentally being pushed along by the wave of air. Instruct the singer to sigh the sustained text "how are you" with considerable inflection. Keep the voice from engaging on its own, avoiding grabbing the sound with the larynx. Using the embouchered facial position referred to in chapter 5 will help keep the sound placed high and out of the throat.

Repeat "how are you" several times, each time slower, stretching out the "are" at the top of the inflection. Now using a similar siren effect with the same lightness and echoey quality, sigh only the word "woe" several times. Gradually use less and less siren glide, and then gently start right on a mid-range pitch, but approaching it still with the sound of the sigh.

SIGH-SINGING

On the syllables "woh-woh-woh___," sigh-sing (singing with the sound of sighing) on pitches 3–2–1—(use the keys of E♭ major, moving up to F major). The airflow and hootiness should be sustained through the final longer note and into the silence. Retaining the same sound and airflow clear through to the silence smoothes out the last note. The normal tendency is to sigh-sing smoothly until the initiation of the last note of the phrase and then unintentionally grab with the larynx, stopping the flow and causing the vibrato problem to reemerge during the long note.

Now expand the same exercise with the pitches 5–4–3–2–1—, using the same suggested keys. Initial notes of any musical phrase need to be gentle and immediately moving forward in the flow, never using a harsh glottal attack. Some type of kinesthetic motion—e.g., the arms making balletlike circles in front of the chest—will help to keep the voice flowing rather than singing note to note.

ADOPTING A NEW CONCEPT

To help the new skill become habitual, the vocalist needs to change his or her concept of what constitutes a healthy singing sound. Instead of the old habit of singing full out in rehearsals (as when helping neighbors find the right notes), singing will henceforth need to be based on sigh-singing. This will take some getting used to and will probably not feel as powerful. But the voice will be more beautiful, more comfortable, and less strained, and with this new sound, the vocalist will be able to enjoy singing for many more years.

CHAPTER 8

OTHER CONCERNS RELATED TO THE VOICE

VISUAL SIGNS OF VOCAL STRAIN

Look up more often to carefully observe your singers during rehearsals. There are times when you can't actually hear that there are vocal problems in your choir, but if you are watching out for it, you can often see the resulting discomfort. Some of the visual signs of vocal strain are:

- tight shoulders and general stiffness
- lack of efficient head and spinal alignment
- pained or uncomfortable facial expressions
- bulging veins in the neck and super-red faces
- tight jaws

Once you see signs of vocal strain, you may be able to solve the problems of several individuals by having the entire choir go through a short process of loosening up their vocal articulators, adjusting their spinal and head alignment, and getting their breath moving (see chapters 1, 2, and 4). Then have your singers assume a pleasant, relaxed facial expression and, *without changing that relaxed facial expression*, sing a medium range, simple "ah." It is almost impossible to make a strained vocal sound while retaining a relaxed, peaceful visage, because if the voice tries to initiate sound in an overly muscular way, the face automatically grimaces. If a peaceful expression is maintained, the sound tends to be far simpler and easier to produce.

Muscular singing, although made with great physical effort, generally lacks resonance and clarity. Carrying power in a voice comes from forward tone placement, not from extreme muscular effort. Once the vocal strain in a few individuals has been eased by having the whole choir go through the above process, it is wise to follow up privately with those most entrenched in these bad habits to reinforce concepts of healthy singing.

Avoid working with an individual's vocal concerns in front of the choir. The voice is personal. It is not a separate object on which we play, such as a violin, but it is rather a part of who we are. When a conductor makes a negative comment about someone's voice, it is bound to hurt feelings, because it feels as if you are saying that there is something wrong with the person. Deal with the voice in private and with great sensitivity.

HOW TO TEACH VOCAL CONCEPTS WHEN YOU DON'T HAVE A GOOD VOICE

The best vocal coaches for professional singers are usually pianists who don't consider themselves singers. Even if you are primarily a pianist or organist, you can read the chapters in this first part of the book and gain a better understanding of the basics. Your first tool of analysis is your eyes. Notice posture and alignment. Help your singers learn better habits of breathing and airflow. With little actual singing expertise, you can learn to illustrate this process effectively.

If you become aware of vocal strain in one of your choir members but don't know immediately what the cause is or how to go about fixing it, you may have to first experience the problem in your own voice. Try to get your voice to imitate exactly the sound you hear in the other voice. Then feel where the tension is in your own throat when you make that sound. Experiment with what you have to do to get rid of that tension. For example, you have a choir member whose voice is throaty and dark, and you make your voice sound the same way, you should notice that your larynx feels jammed down, your voice seems squeezed out of a small space, and you are using little airflow. Alternate tensing and relaxing your throat until you can identify exactly where the tension is. Then practice inhaling and singing without this abnormal pushing down of the larynx. You now have a firsthand understanding of where your choir member's vocal tension is and how to ease it. Follow up by reading the chapters of this book on tone placement (5) and airflow (4).

Using this kind of common sense to come up with practical solutions to vocal concerns is a good first step, but it would be a significant advantage to you as a conductor to invest in voice lessons with a good voice teacher, one with credentials and references. Although it is possible to gain some understanding of the fundamentals of healthy vocal production on your own, certain key concepts need the input of a professional. Experiencing what an open throat and forward tone placement really mean, how they feel, and how they change the sound of your voice, requires the guidance of a good a voice teacher. Invest in voice lessons, not with the goal of becoming a great singer, but simply of being able to model a free, well-supported and well-placed vocal sound. Get that image of vocal production across to them, and the sound of your choir will grow exponentially.

WHEN BOYS' VOICES BEGIN TO CHANGE

Boys whose voices are about to change or are in the midst of change require more oversight than any other singers. Although there are many charts explaining various categories of changing voices, boys seldom remain in any one category for long enough to make that useful. Still, there do seem to be some universal truths.

1. For boys whose voices are about to change or are in the midst of change, you must always be aware of what pitches they can actually sing. This requires checking their high and low notes every couple of weeks, and making sure the notes you are asking them to sing are possible notes for them. The typical changing boys in my middle-school choirs have included:

   - some unchanged trebles who sing soprano
   - some barely changed trebles who sing alto
   - some high tenors (G_3 to A_4, with the most effective pitches being D_4 to F_4)
   - some limited range tenors (F_3 to C_4, with the most effective pitches being G_3 to B_3)
   - some baritones (C_3 to D_4, with the most effective pitches being F_3 to C_4)
   - some basses (G_2 to A_3, with the most effective pitches being C_3 to G_3)

   Every group of changing boys will have a slightly different mix of ranges, including some in categories beyond those listed here. The above categories, however, illustrate the complications of finding music just right for such a complex variety of ranges. For instance, the only notes the nontreble voices (bottom four categories) shared were G_3 to C_4, and even those notes were uncomfortably high for some and too low for others. Having the tenors, baritones, and basses sing in unison was definitely out. The high tenors were most effective in their upper notes, especially around F_4, and therefore limited-range parts within those most effective pitches were perfect. Open fifths between the basses/baritones and the tenors worked well, but only if the pitches were fairly high in the pitch range of each part. Parallel octaves could also be effective, but limited to C up to G, a cumulative range of only a perfect fifth.

2. This information means that music for this age requires more boys' voice parts rather than less. SAB music is rarely useful, as seen from the combination of ranges above. Think about the typical range of an SAB anthem for the boys and compare that to the most effective pitches above. Two-thirds of the boys in the typical middle-school choir suggested above would have few notes they could possibly sing. To be useful for this age choir, music must be easy to adapt to your particular needs. Limited range canons work well. The tenors, baritones, and basses can often sing in octaves, or sometimes a limited-range voice part can sing one section of the canon that lays within their most effective range over and over while the rest of the choir sings the whole canon. Try writing ostinatos for the boys using each part's most effective pitches, creating an effective contrast to the treble voices above. Whatever you create for the changing boys to sing, try to use predominantly the pitches they can sing with the most confidence. For instance, the high tenors can usually sing a G_3, but they cannot project well any pitch below a D_4. When a young boy tries to sing a note below his most effective pitches too loudly, he is in danger of damaging his voice. The notes you ask changing boys to sing need to give them the greatest chance for success and the feeling that they are contributing something special.

PART II

CONDUCTOR PROCEDURES, PREPARATION, AND PLANNING

INTRODUCTION: SELF-PREPARATION OF THE CONDUCTOR

A choral performance should display the result of careful self-preparation by the choral conductor who, in turn, has thoroughly prepared the choir, imparting technical training, stylistic interpretation, and insight into the nature of the music. The conductor's self-preparation begins with the choice of repertoire, which is paramount to a successful choir season. This second part of *The Choral Challenge* provides a guide for how to choose repertoire of quality, of long-term usefulness, and of appeal to both audiences and choir, repertoire that includes a variety of styles and historical periods and takes into account an appropriate difficulty level for your particular choir. Knowledge of the ever-expanding repertoire is essential to the professional choral conductor and teacher, and requires attention and development throughout a career. This means that new ground is often being broken, bringing with it the risks and delights that come with first performances of repertoire, as well as growing ability and discernment.

Equal in importance to the choice of repertoire is the next logical concern: the conductor's comprehensive knowledge of the score. Only a superficial understanding can be gained by playing through the music on the piano, so one needs to embrace an effective analytical procedure for approaching a new score or revisiting known scores. You will find such a procedure for effective score study in chapter 11.

Next is a discussion of how to plan an effective rehearsal. Once that aforementioned score study has been completed, the conductor should be able to ascertain the specific problems unique to each piece of music, what I call the "unique musical focus" (UMF) of a piece. That information, when added to what you already know to be your choir's weaker technical skills, will indicate vocal or musical factors that need special attention and perhaps some preparatory work in the rehearsal. Now suitable warm-up and mid-rehearsal corrective exercises can be chosen specifically for that music and that choir. It is a relatively simple matter to choose exercises that address those highlighted concerns from among the sixty-two exercises included.

This second part also includes a quick and effective procedure for placing singers into correct voice parts at the first of each season, and how to go about teaching mini–voice lessons to all choir members early in the season. There are also ideas for energizing rehearsals and for solving an array of vexing rehearsal concerns. Part 2 ends with a candid and intriguing discussion of the difference in conducting singers versus conducting instrumentalists. The expectations that instrumentalists have of a conductor are surprisingly different from the expectations of singers.

Good performances are not an accident. They are the direct result of a conductor's vocal knowledge, thorough score study and rehearsal planning, and one's ability to analyze and adjust the choral sound to a high ideal.

CHAPTER 9

HOW TO PLACE SINGERS INTO CORRECT VOICE PARTS

If the choir is new to you, particularly if it is a youth choir, less-experienced adult choir, or even a children's choir, there are two time-efficient and remarkably accurate procedures for assigning voice parts. The first is a quick group check, which can be accomplished in the first part of the first rehearsal of the season. This should be followed by short, individual hearings to fine-tune those decisions. As many as a third of the singers in many volunteer choirs are not singing in the section that is best suited to their voices or most helpful to the choir. Often when they first joined a choir, no one actually placed them in a section. They sat with someone they knew and never changed. When choir members are placed into vocal sections that give their voices the best chance of expression and vitality, the whole sound of the choir takes on new life.

THE QUICK GROUP CHECK

Especially for choirs with whom you haven't worked before and for all youth choirs every year, have all the women or girls stand in a semicircle in any order. Beginning with the last person on one end, have each say with a full sound, "Hi, how are you?" one after the other. Simply listen the first time through. Then repeat the process more slowly, allowing some time between each person. After listening to each voice, physically change where that person is standing in the semicircle, moving those with heavier or lower speaking voices toward one end and those with lighter, higher voices to the other end. The goal is to get the singers lined up light to heavy (high to low) completely according to the sound of their speaking voice. You will need to go back and forth between some of the speaking voices and change them back and forth until you are sure. Up to this point, you should not even consider their eventual voice part classification.

Now you begin the process of dividing up the sides to achieve choral balance. Divide the semicircle exactly in two, having the lower, heavier side sing the vowel /ɑ/ (as in "father") on the pitch Ab_4 at a *mezzo-forte* dynamic level, while the higher, lighter side sings C_5. Then have the two sides sing the pitches D_4 and A_4. These two intervals should be a clear indicator of whether the balance is good between the divisions. If it is not well balanced, move a few middle singers from one side to the other as necessary and repeat the intervals until the balance is what you want.

For women or girls, many of those in the middle range could very well sing either second soprano or first alto without vocal concerns. That allows some flexibility in those middle voices to help balance sight-reading and musical leadership. So before going further, ask each person in the semicircle to indicate on their raised fingers how many years of private *instrumental* lessons each have had. This gives you a sense of how many secure music readers are in each of the two divisions. Asking how well they think they sight-read doesn't provide any useful information, as singers rarely are realistic about their own reading proficiency. Private *voice* lessons do not indicate secure music reading skills in the same way as instrumental lessons, since it is less likely that instrumentalists learn by rote. Take a look at the raised fingers to get a sense of whether the soprano or the alto side needs more music reading leadership, and then adjust some of the middle singers with more reading experience up or down as needed. This way every vocal section is not only well balanced but has music reading leadership, which will help immeasurably in the pace of music learning.

Now comes the moment when negotiation is often required. You have determined that this balance of sopranos and altos is good, but you have not accepted input from the choir members. Inevitably there are singers who insist they should be in the other section than the one suggested by this procedure. If they are currently taking voice lessons and their private teacher feels strongly that they should be singing the other voice part, it is probably best to accede to their wishes, unless it is clearly a problem to the sound of the choir. (Mezzo-sopranos, heavier alto quality with a soprano range, should almost always sing alto in a choir.) If the questioning singer, on the other hand, has simply always sung the other voice part and is hesitant about the change, make a deal with them. You certainly don't want to ruin anyone's enjoyment of singing. Ask if they would be willing to give the new voice part a two-week trial. If after that time they still want to switch back, tell them they can make that call, but you feel there is an even chance that they may find the new voice part is a perfect fit. In most cases, they find increased effectiveness and comfort level in the new part and are pleased to stay there.

Now that you have made the above adjustments to your original soprano-alto balance, rehear the intervals above and make sure the balance is still good. Then assign voice classifications using S1, S2, A1, and A2, even if your choir is too small to sing in eight parts. This allows you, for example, to augment an important low phrase in the soprano part by adding all A1s for a few measures.

At this point, the women or girls sit down and the men or boys move into the semicircle, going through the same "Hi, how are you?" process described above. The decisions are generally more self-evident with men and boys, because speaking-voice ranges and quality are better indicators than for women. Although this classification seems clear from their speaking voices, there often seems to be a bass or two who are sure they should be singing tenor and vice versa. Trust the sound of the speaking voice to guide you in voice part classification. Remember that voice classification is not primarily about vocal range but about the quality and the weight of the voice. If you allow a heavy baritone to sing tenor because he can hit all the notes, the choral sound will never balance and the tenor section will usually flat.

For the average-sized choir, the entire "Quick Group Check" process should be able to be accomplished in fifteen minutes for the women or girls, and slightly less time for the men or boys. The same process could be used to divide up the voices in a children's choir. Within the first thirty minutes of the first rehearsal of the season, you have a well-balanced choir with stable music readers in each section.

INDIVIDUAL MINI–VOICE CHECKS

Follow the above quick group check with individual mini–voice checks. These may not be necessary for all choir members but may be significant for the middle voices (S2, A1, T2, B1), singers who seem to have the capacity to sing up or down. Five or six minutes apiece for these individual voice checks should be plenty of time. The idea is to determine in what range they are most comfortable and have the most to offer the choir.

Begin by checking the size and sound of their voices in moderately low and high ranges. Have them sing the pitches 1–2–3–2–1 on a sustained /ɑ/ (as in "father") at a *mezzo forte* dynamic level, first beginning on middle C (C_4), and then beginning on A_4 (for men and boys, one octave lower). Ask which is most comfortable for them. Then have them sing the first phrase of "My Country, 'Tis of Thee" ("My country, 'tis of thee, sweet land of liberty, of thee I sing") in the keys of C, F, and B♭ (above). If they are most comfortable and sound best in the lower key of C, they are most likely second altos or basses. If the key of F is best for them, they are probably first altos (unless their voice quality is very lyric) or baritones. If the higher key of B♭ is most comfortable, they are most likely tenors or sopranos. Listen carefully and follow your instincts. Comfort level when using an open-throated full sound is the most significant factor.

CHAPTER 10

CONSIDERATIONS IN CHOOSING REPERTOIRE

There is a better way to choose music. Most of us have attended choral reading sessions, enjoying the chance to sing for a change, and hoping that some piece of music will "knock our socks off!" Often, on the spur of the moment and inspired by the sound of all those directors singing their hearts out, we buy a few pieces that struck us as either pretty or exciting, putting them on the shelves beside the pretty and exciting choices from the last reading session. Since the choice of music has so much to do with the way the choir feels and its eventual success, consider making that choice in a more careful, deliberate way. When you attend your next choral reading session, go through the following checklist before you make your decisions:

1. Does the music have anything *immediately intriguing* about it that grabs your interest? Although important, this has too often been the only criterion for choosing repertoire.

2. Is the *text* useful, interesting, and, for church musicians, theologically sound?

3. Is the *melody* interesting? Does it have anything enticing about it? Is it a tune that stays in your head?

4. Is the *harmony* interesting or plain? Does the harmony lead your ears forward, pulling you along and making you yearn for what is to come?

5. Is the *accompaniment* effective, without being overpowering to the voices?

6. Are the *ranges* of the choral parts appropriate for and singable by your choir?

7. Is there an appropriate *level of complexity* for your choir? Will the effort and time it takes to learn the piece be worth the result?

8. Even if your choir cannot sing the music exactly as written, is the music *adaptable* for use by your particular choir? Are all the parts necessary, or can the accompaniment or other available instruments cover voice parts missing in your choir?

9. If you have a situation in which you can't guarantee a full choir for every performance, can this music be *simplified* if necessary?

CHAPTER 11

CONDUCTOR STUDY PROCEDURES

OVERVIEW

You see both kinds. There are some conductors whose musical preparation is excellent, but they do not spend the administrational time required for a healthy, thriving choir program. They have much they could teach, but not many singers show up. On the other side of things, there are those conductors who are exceptionally well-organized administrators and recruiters, but they run out of time before they get to their own musical preparation. Regardless of the reason, when a conductor hasn't studied enough to unlock the musical intrigue inherent in the music to be rehearsed, rehearsals become drudgery—tedious, note-learning sessions. People don't sing in choirs to learn notes. They yearn to experience the beauty of how those notes are put together. When rehearsals are interesting and artistic, learning notes is a pleasure.

Administrate or study? You don't have to choose. Conductors can and need to do both, but such balance requires the efficient use of the always-limited time available for study. It is not adequate preparation to play through the music once or twice on the piano, because that doesn't show you what the choir members experience in rehearsals. Playing through on the piano won't unlock the secrets that lead to rehearsals that are interesting to the singers.

A conductor should look at the music from the singers' perspective. What will they be looking at and hearing? How do they find their entry pitches? What should they be more aware of? Who has the melody and should therefore be predominant? Who is in a supportive role and should therefore back off? When do various voice parts share little duets and should therefore listen to one another? What is the style of articulation (legato, marcato, staccato), and does it ever change? Where are the climaxes in each phrase, and where does each phrase relax? What are the inherent enunciation dangers? Where should the singers breathe and are those decisions uniform among the voice parts? What is the dramatic mood of the music? Does the overall dynamic level ever change?

Effective study procedures uncover ways to be more time efficient in rehearsals. By figuring out the form of the music, sections that are an exact repeat need not be rehearsed twice. Variations of sections can be rehearsed together with the original, having the choir mark where the first difference occurs, the place they will most likely become derailed. Awkward entrances can be isolated, with suggestions of how to find those pitches. Most likely note problems can be circled in advance in the conductor's score, speeding the process and clarity of corrections.

The time commitment for this type of score study is not as overwhelming as it may appear, because not every piece of music for every rehearsal has to be studied with such care. Once your personal copy of the music is marked thoroughly (as suggested below), it is a far quicker procedure to review those notes before subsequent rehearsals. Except for the first rehearsals of each season, you should have to study in depth only one or two new pieces or movements before each rehearsal. The other music for the rehearsal should be music studied and marked carefully in subsequent weeks, which means a simple review from earlier notes. Then year to year, the percentage of your scheduled music for which you have such carefully marked and studied personal copies grows steadily. Rehearsals become less time consuming to prepare for, more effective, and more enticing to the choir.

A PROCEDURE FOR SCORE STUDY

1. Read the text without regard for the music. It is a good idea to type out the text separately, marking probable breathing places based simply upon making the text clear. Look up and note any questionable words or references (choir members are bound to ask). Also note larger divisions (paragraphs) in the text.

2. Transfer those probable breathing places to each voice part in the score. Then slightly adjust those breath marks if it allows several voice parts to breathe at the same time. Staggered breathing gives a pleasing effect, but it also often robs music of the natural ebb and flow (arsis and thesis) that textual breathing offers choral music.

3. Determine the large and small structural divisions based primarily upon the textual analysis above. Count the measures in each division and put them in order on a

separate sheet of paper—e.g., introduction, 4 measures; A section, 8 measures; B section, 8 measures; interlude, 2 measures; A section, 8 measures; etc. If the divisions are mathematically simple, a quick memorization of the form allows you to conduct almost from memory except for the sections where your analysis (see no. 5 below) indicates the need for closer attention to the score. These musical divisions are also useful as places to start and stop when working a section at a time in rehearsals.

4. Determine the key and if it ever changes. Knowing what the tonic looks and sounds like can be a significant asset in the choir's reading stability. Key changes often throw up caution flags for concerns about transition notes, as well as occasionally indicating a change of style or dramatic mood.

5. Sight-sing each part by itself. Sit at the piano, but don't play along while you sing. Use the piano only to check for accuracy. Sight-singing the voice parts shows you which notes are most likely to be stumbling blocks for your choir members. Circle each likely note of concern, placing an arrow up or down above the circle indicating which direction choir members need to push the note to be accurate. During rehearsal, listen carefully as these probable note concerns are approached, and if they occur, immediately suggest that choir members put in their scores the arrow visual aids you have in yours. There is a 95 percent chance that any notes missed will be those you anticipated. Circling probable note concerns protects you from the tendency of singers to fade out when unsure of a pitch. You might never hear a wrong note because they didn't sing anything and the piano accompaniment filled in the correct note. When the problem is finally uncovered, it is often too late in the game to be dealing with wrong notes. If you have the note marked as a probable concern, you can't be tricked.

6. Look through the score. When more than one part has a note circled in one chord, meaning multiple probable note concerns, put a vertical box around the whole chord. Then before the choir sings through that section for the first time, isolate that problem. Move back a measure from that boxed chord and lead one part at a time into it, sustaining its pitch in the chord of concern. Then add one more part; then, another. The same layering technique can be used for finding the initial pitches in any new section. Finding correct first pitches is always a primary consideration.

7. Note when any voice part has not been singing for a measure or more, and circle or highlight its next entrance. Getting back in after a rest is much more difficult than keeping one's place when singing.

8. Note the highpoints of the first several phrases in each voice part. These can be marked with a curved arrow from the first note of the phrase to the climax of the phrase (the arsis), after which the phrase begins to relax (the thesis). The climax of the phrase is often not the highest pitch in the phrase; it is generally two-thirds of the way through the phrase and is often a note later than the obvious place. Targeting an emphasis further down the phrase helps choirs sing *through* the phrase instead of *to* the climax. Once the choir experiences this expressive style of phrase contouring in their first several phrases, they should be able to retain the style on their own through the rest of the composition.

9. Now look at the vocal parts in their relationship to one another. See where various vocal sections sing duets or trios with one another and bracket them. Isolate these parts in rehearsal, asking that the singers listen to one another and work together musically. Again, not all vocal parts are equally important throughout a composition, so decide what you want to be proportionally more dominant. A singer should then be constantly shifting gears in the music between "here I lead out" and "now I'm in a supportive role." The conductor's score should include angled lines leading their eyes from one predominant vocal part to another, especially in complex music.

10. Determine if there are musical themes, melodic fragments that are repeated elsewhere in the composition, perhaps in other choral parts. Highlight the theme wherever it occurs, using a second color for secondary themes. This is most easily noted during the sight-singing of each vocal part (see no. 5 above). A highlighted theme in your score means that proportionally that vocal part must have slightly more dominance than the other parts. If the tessitura of the theme in that part is low and the accompanying parts higher, more of a difference needs to be made dynamically between the voice parts. Trust your ear to guide your proportions. Borrow some singers from another voice part to augment the theme as necessary. The dynamics marked in the score are simply guidelines.

11. At the beginning of a composition in the margin above or to the left of the music, put a large box that includes the meter,

the tempo, and the opening dynamic level. This is a quick reminder of the basics. If the treatment of the dynamics is complex—e.g., subito changes in dynamics between sections as in music of the Baroque or Classical eras (terraced dynamics)—color code the dynamics. Circle any dynamic symbol of *mezzo forte* and louder with red ink and *mezzo piano* and quieter with blue ink. Crescendos are underlined in red; diminuendos, in blue. Subito changes receive a vertical line through all the parts with the upcoming dynamic's color. The markings are an easy-to-see shorthand in the score, a reminder to pay attention to the dynamics.

12. Translate exactly any Italian or other musical terms. Don't guess. Look them up and write the translations in the score.

13. Determine the mode of articulation that would be most effective with that composition—e.g., legato, staccato, marcato, portato. If there is a contrasting section, the mode of articulation may change. The mode of articulation is often not indicated in the score, but the conductor should always let the choir know what style to use. Note that staccato is most effective in *piano* dynamic levels and marcato with *forte* dynamics.

14. Check the exact tempo with a metronome. It is a good place to start, although your musical instincts, your sensitivity to your own choir, and acoustics need to be the ultimate determinants. The Italian or other nonnumeric tempo suggestions—e.g., *andante*—are often more insightful in gaining the results hoped for by the composer. If it feels rushed, it is not *andante*.

15. Highlight meter or tempo changes within the composition, including ritards, accelerandos, and fermatas.

16. Where there are multiple tempos within a composition— e.g., in a major work—copy the meters on a separate sheet in performance order. Using a Tempowatch™ or a metronome, practice finding each tempo, in performance order, one after the other.

17. In a large-scale work with soloists, determine and mark in your score standing and seating directions, and whether they will be by cue from the conductor or at an exact place in the music.

18. Check to see that all choir members have the same edition of the music. If not, number your measures (every ten measures or at the beginning of each system), or put rehearsal letters

at obvious structural divisions, which can be quickly given out to the choir. Conductor and choir must be able to find the place quickly and efficiently.

19. Research information on the composer, the author of the text, the time and place where the composition was written, what life was like when the composition was first performed—anything that might add some intrigue to that music. No lengthy lectures—just tidbits of intrigue to peak the curiosity of the singers. Simon & Schuster, Inc., publishes a book by Bernard Grun called *The Timetables of History: A Horizontal Linkage of People and Events*, which describes what life was like in each decade from A.D. 400 to the present. It is fascinating to choir members to imagine life at another time and its relationship to a piece of music they are singing.

CHAPTER 12

WARM-UP EXERCISES

OVERVIEW

There is no getting around it. The first ten minutes of rehearsals can be frustrating and are often ineffective. Conductors are eager to get started but hesitate because of so many late arrivals. Singers who did arrive on time become frustrated that rehearsal is starting late, wondering why they made the effort to be prompt. When things do finally get under way, it seems a long time before actual singing begins, which is what they really came for. Instead, the conductor makes announcements, vents frustration about late arrivals and no-shows, and then launches into the same old tedious warm-up exercises, regardless of what music is ahead. By the time choir members get to sing real music, it is often fifteen minutes into rehearsal, and they are no better prepared vocally or musically than they were before rehearsal started. The enthusiasm they initially brought into the rehearsal room has begun to sag.

So how can you make the first ten minutes of rehearsal more enjoyable and effective, and thereby increase people's desire to arrive on time? One way is to begin rehearsals with singing instead of talking. Adopt a default opening sequence, beginning with singing the same chorale, spiritual, canon, or verse of a favorite hymn at each rehearsal. You can use standard harmonizations, or even let the choir improvise on a well-known tune, such as "Swing Low, Sweet Chariot." Within a few rehearsals of starting this way, the music should be memorized, allowing it to be sung without the complication of getting music out, even by those just coming in the door. This opening music should be relatively short, enjoyable to sing, lovely to hear, and preferably quiet and sustained. Don't rehearse it; just let the choir sing. No one wants to miss singing this beautiful opening music, which occurs only once each rehearsal and begins exactly on time, and therefore singers work harder to be prompt and immediately engaged.

Once the traditional opening piece has been sung, take just a bit of time to loosen up the body and the vocal apparatus, get your singers into better spinal alignment, get their breath moving, and remind them about forward tone placement (see the related chapters on the voice in part 1). These physical and vocal reminders can soon become a quick, automatic part of your choir's opening calisthenics, led mostly by gesture. Each of these basics will need reinforcement throughout each rehearsal as well.

Now have the choir take out the first music scheduled to be rehearsed. Let them read through the whole piece one time without stopping to correct anything. Just let them sing. Don't underestimate how much people love to sing. The inevitable starting and stopping of cleaning up musical details too early in the rehearsal is hard to take first thing when what people really want to do is sing. If choir members begin to believe that the first part of rehearsal will have more singing and less listening to the conductor talk, they will work harder to get there on time.

So, in the first six minutes of rehearsal the choir has sung a beautiful "theme song," been reminded of the basics of good vocal technique, and had the chance to really sing for a while without interruption, all in the same time you used to wait for enough choir members to arrive to be able to start. In the new system, those singers who arrive late will miss a good time, but they will not have missed any of your instructions and specific skill building. Motivation is high, and the choir is ready to get down to serious work. Now it is time to revert back to a warm-up that will help refine that first piece that you just sang through.

But which warm-up exercise should you use? Why bother doing them at all? What are warm-ups supposed to accomplish? Why take the time? The problem is that choir directors often use exercises that their conductors or voice teachers used with them. The choir you conduct now, however, probably has different problems than the one you used to sing in, and to make matters more complex, each piece of music brings its own skill or stylistic challenges. The obvious answer is that, in order to be effective, warm-up exercises must be chosen to match the problems inherent in your choir and the music to be rehearsed.

DETERMINING YOUR NEEDS

1. Based upon your general knowledge of your choir and from the last rehearsal or performance, what skills does your choir most need work on?

   - Do they tend to sing flat?
   - Do they have trouble with agility?
   - Do they have clear enunciation?

- Do they need to sing with more energy?
- Do they have trouble blending in quieter music?
- Do they need to widen their palette of dynamics?
- Do they need to shape their phrases more effectively?
- Do they need to work on tuning chords?

2. Next, what are the inherent musical or vocal challenges in each piece of music you plan to rehearse? I call these "UMFs," a "unique musical focus" for each piece of music. Since there are multiple challenges in every piece of music, list several of the most obvious on the first page of the music, under the heading UMF. Some examples:

   - Make the third beat in a $\frac{3}{4}$ meter pull into the first beat.
   - Modify spread "eh" vowels.
   - Adjust the proportions in a fugal section so that the theme can be heard.
   - Tune the third of a major chord high enough.
   - Note legato vs. marcato articulation styles.
   - Use agogic delays for text emphasis.

   Look at all the pieces to be rehearsed. From the UMF choices you have already listed at the beginning of each piece of music, choose one on which to concentrate, different for each piece of music to be rehearsed in that rehearsal. Such variety of teaching concepts keeps your rehearsals more interesting.

3. Now that you know what skills need to be honed for both your choir and the music scheduled, it is time to match up those needs with exercises that teach those specific skills. In order to find appropriate choices, analyze every choral or vocal exercise you know *by its function*. The sixty-two warm-up exercises in this chapter are already identified in this way. Effective exercises should not only teach specific skills, but they should be moderately short and easy to teach. An exercise shouldn't take more than five minutes of rehearsal time. Increased complexity is not an asset, even for an advanced choir. Two-part mixed exercises teach just as effectively as four- and eight-part exercises, but require much less time to make the point and teach the skill. I don't know any conductors who feel they have enough rehearsal time, so teaching concepts quickly and getting on to the music sooner is an asset. Remember that these exercises can be used either as warm-ups or as mid-rehearsal corrective exercises, so beside each UMF factor that you listed on the first page of the music, now identify a functionally related exercise you can use as needed.

4. You have chosen the perfect exercises for your choir and the music; now do them exactly right. Care about detail. Instead of staring at the music, look intently at your choir. Notice their stance, their breathing, and their physical involvement. Listen to their precision, tone color, and tuning. Really build the skill intended by your choice of that exercise. Then go quickly into the music, intentionally carrying the skills learned from the exercise into the next part of the rehearsal. Don't be casual in the time between finishing the exercise and starting to work on the music. Remind the choir of the skills they just learned and challenge them to carry those skills into the music. They will not get tired of the single-minded focus on this music, because as soon as they finish working on that piece, the UMF will change for the next selection of music, and the new focus will create its own freshness.

62 FUNCTIONAL

KEY WORD	FUNCTION	EXERCISE
1. agility	developing agility through staccatos	*Swedish "yah-hahs"*: Good spinal alignment and an open throat are essential; the breath support and resulting airflow do not change between the staccatos or through the longer notes; each measure is one long breath support, not individual attacks; let the belly relax completely on breaths between the measures, and then resupport; repeat up by half steps.
2. agility	developing agility in the low register	*Descending scale with trill on last note*: Breath support must be consistent throughout; the sixteenth notes do not affect that; support through the entire last note; make sure the trill is a true whole step; repeat up by half steps.
3. agility	developing agility and a loose jaw	*Agility and loose jaw*: Modify the *ay* vowel toward an *ee* to keep the vowel from spreading; let the jaw flop freely, but not excessively open; repeat up by half steps.
4. agility	developing agility for melismas	*Agility for melismas*: Both of these vowels are formed in the front of the mouth and both have a smallish mouth shape; retain the open nasal feeling from the *n*'s thoughout; keep the breath support consistent throughout; repeat up by half steps.

WARM-UP EXERCISES

(Vocal Health and Pedagogy, p. 325, Robert Thayer Sataloff)

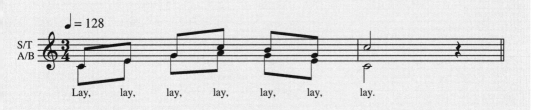

KEY WORD	FUNCTION	EXERCISE
5. agility	alternating staccato and legato; giving direction to note groupings	*Agility and directional flow*: After the first note, all shorter notes pull toward longer notes (e.g., the second and third notes pull toward the fourth); the breath support stays connected even after staccatos; give significance to the final note; repeat up by half steps.
6. articulation	modes of articulation	*Learning articulation modes*: Sing in unison a well-known song (e.g., "Down by the Old Mill Stream" or "It Came upon a Midnight Clear") legato, so connected that the pitches slightly slide; then sing the same song staccato; then have half the choir sing it legato and the other half staccato; ask what the combined sound effect was for a listener; then sing that combination sound, a crisp initiation as in staccato with the smooth follow through of legato (called portato); you might also add marcato (heavy accents without completely detaching between notes).
7. articulators	loosening the tip of the tongue	*Min-min-min*: This exercise is much more effective if the *ih* vowel is modified toward *ee* to focus the sound; an embouchered face is also beneficial; sing with high energy and aggressive style; foot stomping on the first beat of each measure gets singers physically involved; repeat up by half steps, adding an extra foot stomp for the measure between repeats.
8. articulators	loose jaw and open throat	*My mamma's in the Bahamas*: The combination of the opening nasal consonants followed by all the *ah* vowels make this exercise exceptional easy on the throat and freeing to sing; carry the phrase emphasis to the penultimate note; sense vertical vowels filling the mouth; repeat up by half steps.

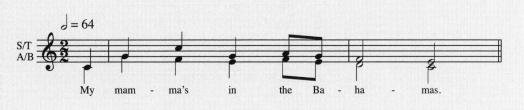

KEY WORD	FUNCTION	EXERCISE
9. articulators	working the lips and tip of the tongue	*You know I love unique New York*: "Unique New York" is hard to say or sing; keep the sound right up the front of your mouth; "New" begins with the vanishing vowel *ee*; for "York" the vowel should be *oh*; repeat up by half steps.
10. blending	procedure for developing blend	*Blending one person at a time*: Begin by having one clear voice in the section sing a mid-range /ɔ/ (as in "jaw"); have one more voice join, adjusting his or her sound to imitate the first voice exactly; then add a third, and so on, until the entire section joins in that quality of sound.
11. break	smoothing the break between the head-tone and chest-tone registers	*Connecting the registers*: Check alignment and use exercises to get the air flowing; hum-sigh or yawn-sigh several times using the kinesthetic device of making small upward circles in front of the sternum with the fingers of both hands, elbows out from the body and finger tips rebounding lightly off the sternum as a reminder to stay connected physically; beginning on an /u/ vowel (as in "soon") with the same light, floating sound, begin the pitches 5–4–3–2–1 in the key of D major; on the way down the scale, gradually open the vowel to /ɔ/ (as in "song") along with a moderate crescendo; then repeat, but this time returning up the scale (5–4–3–2–1–2–3–4–5), gradually changing back to the /u/ vowel and diminuendo on the ascent; keep the airflow ample, especially in the diminuendo.
12. cadences	stretching cadences with agogic delays	*Ensemble in ritardandos*: This exercise helps develop ensemble in cadences of slower, *espressivo* music; beginning at a moderately quick tempo, speak the words "1 and 2 and 3 and 4 and 1—", with the ritardando beginning on "3" and stretching the penultimate word "and" in order to emphasize the final "1" (an agogic delay); then sing the same exercise as written, repeating the phrase up by half steps.

You know I love u - nique New York.

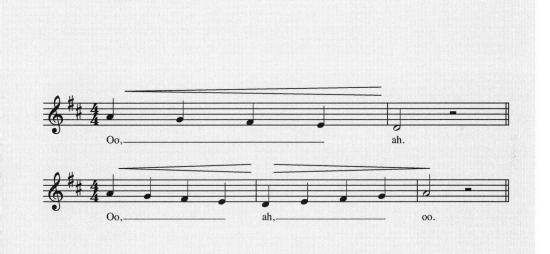

Oo, ah.

Oo, ah, oo.

One and two and three and four and one.

KEY WORD	FUNCTION	EXERCISE
13. chest tone	women and girls developing chest tone	*Chest-tone exercise*: The idea of this exercise is to completely separate head tone and chest tone to help woman and girl singers commit to one or the other in various parts of the range; the initial higher note should be full-throated and hooty, sliding down and breaking on purpose (like a yodel) to vibrant belly laugh staccatos on the bottom; the bottom notes should have forward placement, with the mouth not too open (which would force the larynx too low); as a general rule, women and girls should switch to chest tone when the pitches fall below F_4; repeat down by half steps.
14. concentration	building exactness and mental focus	*Silent singing*: Sing one verse of "My Country, 'Tis of Thee" in unison and legato; then do the same with a quiet staccato; then sing only the first staccato pitch of each measure (silent singing between); then the first of every other measure; then play "Russian roulette," with the director gesturing for a note at any time; the point is building exactness, concentration, and reliance on watching the conductor.

(attributed to Bruce Foote)

KEY WORD	FUNCTION	EXERCISE
15. diction	activating the facial articulators	*Zinga zinga zoo*: The four different sets of words in this exercise are excellent for diction; "zinga" works the nasal consonants; "ticky-tacky," explosive consonants; "yabba-dabba," *b*'s and *d*'s; "waw-daw-waw-daw," *w*'s; the facial articulators must be active; repeat up by half steps.

KEY WORD	FUNCTION	EXERCISE
16. diction	keeping vowels from spreading; modes of articulation	*Bee-ay-bay*: To sing this exercise well, keep in mind that the /e/ vowel (as in "say") is closely related to the /i/ vowel (as in "see"), so when going from /i/ to /e/, don't let your mouth open unnecessarily wide; most of these vowel sounds are made with the front of the mouth, and although the lips are active and the face embouchered, the basic lip and jaw opening is small; learn this exercise slowly and legato, concentrating on keeping the vowel sounds in line; then sing it staccato a little faster; then sing it portato (initiations like a staccato with the smooth follow-through of a legato).
17. diction	vowel color and clarity	*Dickey dwee*: The /ɪ/ vowel (as in "sit") should be produced almost like a small-mouthed, umlauted /i/ (as in "see") to give it focus; keep the air flowing clear through the final note; repeat up by half steps.

Bee - ay - bay, bee - ee - bee, bee - i - bick - ee - by, bee - oh - boh, bick - y - by - boh - bee - oo - boo, bick - ee - by - boh - boo - oo.

(attributed to Weston Noble)

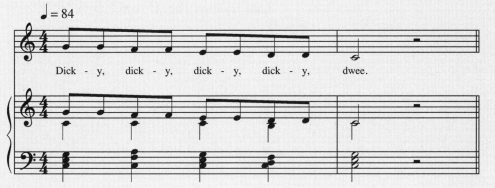

Dick - y, dick - y, dick - y, dick - y, dwee.

KEY WORD	FUNCTION	EXERCISE
18. diction	vowel colors and necessary tongue adjustments	*Aw-ee-aw*: This exercise requires the same vertical, embouchered facial position and jaw opening throughout, while the tongue makes slight adjust-ments in position (see chapter 1); the tip of the tongue should always be forward against the lower teeth; for the *aw* vowel, the tongue is spread wide, touching the lower teeth on both sides and being slightly humped in the back; for the *ee* vowel, the still-forward tongue is narrower, not noticeably touching the teeth on the sides, and humped further forward; using kinesthetic motions can help the learning of this coordination (e.g., putting the hands in front of the shoulders, palms down, spreading the fingers for *aw* and narrowing the finger tips to a round point for *ee*); repeat up by half steps.
19. diction	developing richer vowel sounds	*A little bit British*: Sing the first few phrases of "My Country, 'Tis of Thee" with your best English accent, embouchering up the face, and using a rather small lip shape; slightly umlaut all vowels and modify *ah-ee* diphthongs toward *oi* (i.e., "Moy cawn-try").
20. diction	developing better consonants	*A little bit Italian*: Sing the first few phrases of "My Country, 'Tis of Thee," making an overdone, bad imitation of an Italian accent (i.e., "My-uh_ coun-tuhry-uh_tis_of-uh_thee-uh, sweet-uh_land-uh_of-uh_liberty-uh, ov-uh_Thee-uh_I-uh_sing-uh"); note that all the words are connected, the sound never stops, and the breath support does not diminish when approaching a consonant; sing the song again, this time singing crisp consonants with connectivity and sustained energy.

Aw - ee - aw - ee - aw - ee - aw - ee - aw.

KEY WORD	FUNCTION	EXERCISE
21. diction	developing better consonants	*A consonant happy birthday*: Sound the rhythm of "Happy Birthday" using only the consonants *t*, *p*, or *k*, making sure the explosions are supported and use plenty of air; then with the same rhythm, repeat single-syllable names in your choir, e.g., Tom or Joe; the names should be repeated legato, and the breath support should not diminish from conso-nant to vowel to consonant; then sing the names in that rhythm, with altos and basses on G and sopranos and tenors on B♭.
22. dynamics	determining exact dynamic levels	*Setting dynamic levels*: Sing "aw" on a G pitch (or two-part with sopranos and basses on B♭ and altos and basses on G), gradually crescendo from *piano* to *forte* over eight beats; take a breath and then diminuendo from *forte* to *piano* over eight beats (the diminuendo is more difficult because of the tendency to diminish the airflow); have the choir sing what they think *mezzo forte* would be (with the conductor adjusting as necessary); then *mezzo piano*, *piano*, and *pianissimo*; start again at *mezzo forte* and specify the louder dynamic levels in the same way; when you go back to real music, insist on the exact dynamics you have specified.

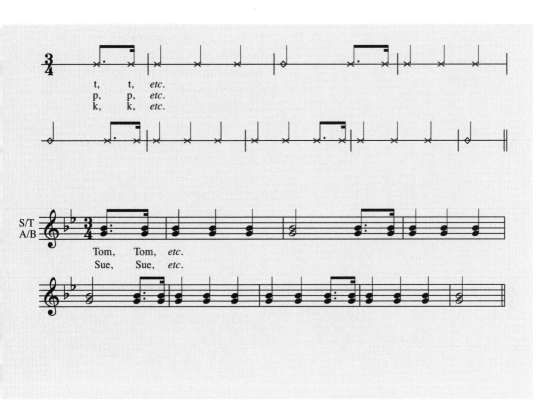

KEY WORD	FUNCTION	EXERCISE
23a. energizer	vocal energizer; resonance builder	*Zinga zinga zoo and variation for two parts*: Begin by swinging arms on quarter-note beats and speaking four spirited, sternum-centered "zings" with siren-like inflection, letting the z consonants provide inertia; now sing the exercise, retaining the movements and the spirited flavor on the first note of each $\frac{3}{4}$ measure (the $\frac{3}{4}$ measure feels in one and the $\frac{2}{4}$ measure in two); the two-part variation in 23b allows sopranos and tenors to sing in a more comfortable range; repeat up by half steps.

KEY WORD	FUNCTION	EXERCISE
23b. energizer	vocal energizer; resonance builder	See 23a.
24. energizer	accented nasal consonants with movements	*Zing-ee zang-ee*: This exercise is driven by accents on each major beat; try walking in place on the beats while singing; sing the final chord full for two beats, adding two beats of rest before repeating up a half step.

KEY WORD	FUNCTION	EXERCISE
25. ensemble	building rhythmic ensemble	*Jungle rhythms*: This exercise was originally only spoken, and that is still how I would start. Give out one section's rhythm (use the ones from the exercise) by rote, having them join in and repeat ad libitum; after a few measures, add a second part; then a third; then a fourth; when all parts have joined, gradually begin changing the tempo by conducting gestures, speeding up and then slowing down, eventually going into eight, and ending with an agogic delay before the final note; experiment with having choir members tap the pulse on their neighbors' shoulders as the tempo changes (this locks in the group's rhythmic ensemble); in a subsequent rehearsal, sing the rhythms as in the exercise.
26. initiations	sensitive initiating of phrases and longer sustained notes	*Naw, naw, naw and variation for four parts*: Starting with the two-part version, begin at *piano* but with ample airflow, crescendoing immediately to *mezzo forte*; at the end of each note, let it go without pulling back or closing down the throat; instruct singers to listen to each other to match crescendos and for tuning; the four-part variation has sopranos and altos (on "noo") respectively an octave and a half above the tenors and basses (on "naw"), reinforcing the overtone series and giving an unusually powerful tuning experience; repeat up by half steps.
27. kinesthetics	kinesthetic motions while singing	*Kinesthetics*: Whether warming up on a variety of exercises or rehearsing actual music, the use of motions loosens the torso, increases the vitality of the voice, and makes the process of breathing more natural and rehearsals more interesting; it is vital to use only motions that allow singers to stay in good alignment, with the top of the spine stretching upwards.

(attributed to Robert Shaw)

KEY WORD	FUNCTION	EXERCISE
28. kinesthetics	example of adding motions	*Zinga zinga zoo*: As an example of adding kinesthetic arm and hand motions to a warm-up exercise, here are some motions you could use with "Zinga zinga zoo" (ex. 23): position the hands comfortably in front of the shoulders as if holding a large ball; in the first $\frac{3}{8}$ measure, flick the fingers of the left hand open energetically on the first beat, letting the hand move forward and ascend slightly; second measure, the right hand; third, left; fourth, right; for the closing $\frac{2}{4}$ measures, flick the left-hand fingers on 1, right-hand fingers on 2, and fingers of both hands on 1 of the last measure; consider also stamping a foot on each of those places, alternating feet left and right to match the hands (but ending with just the left foot).

KEY WORD	FUNCTION	EXERCISE
29. lighter singing	singing at quieter dynamic levels	*Developing the lighter mechanism*: One of the objects of this exercise is to develop a "hootier" mid-range sound for the sopranos and altos; have the men sing the first pitch with a full, round falsetto sound with support and high placement, and then have the sopranos and altos imitate that sound exactly; now sing the exercise as written, insisting on ample airflow and forward placement; the men should retain that lighter-weight sound when they get into their normal range; repeat down by half steps until F major.

(attributed to John Yarrington)

KEY WORD	FUNCTION	EXERCISE
30. listening	group building; listening skills	*Tone cluster exercise (attributed to Robert Shaw)*: Make sure no music is being played before rehearsal starts, which would give the subconscious ear a sense of key; after explanations, on a signal from the conductor, choir members should start singing on /u/ (as in "soon") any pitch that comes to mind (not extremely high or low), retaining exactly that initial pitch regardless of what they hear around them; on a second signal, each singer lets his or her pitch glide slightly higher or lower in pitch until there is some sense of a relationship with some other pitch in the room (this relationship could be any interval); do not intentionally build specific chords; once that relationship is discerned, lock into that pitch and quit moving, waiting for the other pitches to settle; this is an effective way to "come together" musically and in terms of focus.
31. louder	building a heavier, louder vocal quality	Jaws *theme*: Begin by speaking several ascending mid-range "yips," using an umlauted sound and good breath support; then sing the same sound, begin on a G pitch, sliding slowly up half steps (as in the *Jaws* theme), carrying the lower note power into the upper note; then sing just the upper note with the weight of the lower pitch.
32. mental	mental stimulator	*1–2–3's*: Say the staccato word "flip," making it a quick upward motion in the throat; using the same style, say the numbers "one, two, three, four" as if enunciating each one separately, each with its own inflection; now sing the exercise with that type of articulation, but at a *piano* dynamic level; the first time sing all the numbers *piano*; the second time, sing the number "1" *forte*, with all the other numbers still sung *piano*; sing a third time, this time sing the same accenting on the way up, but when the groupings go to 1–2–3–4's, continue to accent each third item, regardless of number or pitch; con-duct the $\frac{6}{8}$ measures in one and the $\frac{2}{4}$ measures in two.

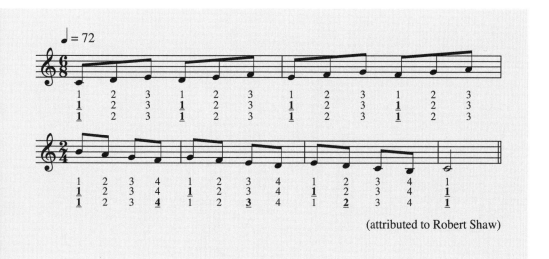

(attributed to Robert Shaw)

KEY WORD	FUNCTION	EXERCISE
33. phrasing	targeting phrase climaxes	*Dona eis Domine*: This teaches targeting a specific note in a phrase as the high point of the trajectory; when singing the first pitch, already be thinking about and aiming for the first beat of the second measure; more than a crescendo, it is a "yearning" of the phrase to go there; in the actual music following this exercise, have the choir circle these target notes throughout at least one section, and work at bringing out the "arsis and thesis," the ebb and flow, of the phrase; repeat up by half steps.
34. phrasing	targeting for effective phrasing and *espressivo*; "arsis and thesis"	*Mary, Mary, Mary*: Sing this exercise legato through-out, with the momentum of the first measure leaning into ("arsis") the third beat and relaxing ("thesis") on the fourth beat; in the second measure, lean in again to the expressive first note and relax on the second note; the first vowel of "Mary" must be /e/ (as in "say"), which is related to /i/ as in "see," not the more spread mouthed /æ/ (as in "sat"); in other words, the face embouchure and shape of the lips does not change perceptibly in this exercise; a slight portamento up into the last measure adds color and expressivity if done with taste; repeat up by half steps.

Do - na e - is, Do - mi - ne.

Ma - ry, Ma - ry, Ma - ry, Ma - ry.

(attributed Frauke Haasemann)

KEY WORD	FUNCTION	EXERCISE
35. phrasing	targeting for effective phrasing and *espressivo*; "arsis and thesis"	*"All through the Night" and variation for two parts*: This serenely beautiful lullaby is a perfect warm-up; the listed vowel sounds add to the effect of the "arsis and thesis," the ebb and flow, of the phrase; the closed vowels make the line more smooth; the second part of the variation adds a little more interest and allows the repeating by half steps to go much higher.
36. phrasing	discovering the sound of momentum	*Minor blues phrase momentum*: The last note of the first measure pulls strongly toward the next measure, creating natural momentum; that is the feeling we want on all notes in effective legato singing; the "oo" leads smoothly into the word "waw"; repeat up by half steps.

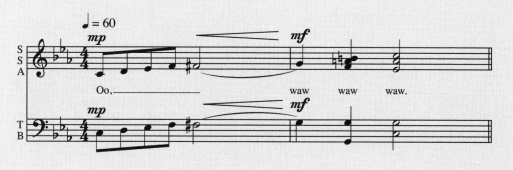

KEY WORD	FUNCTION	EXERCISE
37. pick-ups	creating directional momentum	*Anacruses momentum*: Singing short notes in such a way that they have forward momentum into the following longer notes adds vitality and momentum to the music; target the first beat of the second measure as the high point in the phrase, which then relaxes; the crescendos and diminuendos add to the effect; having the sopranos and altos alternate with the tenors and basses makes an effective switching of the aural spotlight; the beginning of each crescendo should start from nothing, and the end of each diminuendo should almost disappear; go directly into a piece of music that has a lot of shorter notes leading into longer ones.
38. pitch	developing pitch sensitivity	*Gradual pitch changing*: Have the choir begin on the mid-range G with a *mezzo piano* /u/ vowel (as in "soon") and imperceptibly raise the pitch, arriving at G♯ in about twelve seconds; then sing the first G with that same feeling of raising the pitch, but never quite leaving the G; this creates buoyancy and precision pitch sensitivity; ample, steady airflow and breath support is essential.
39. pitch	pitch sensitivity	*Whole tone canon*: Slowly hum up and back down the five-note whole-tone scale, being particularly careful of the pitch-sensitive fourth degree; then do the same again as a two-part canon, with the second part entering as the first part begins the second measure; sing slowly enough that the major seconds can be continuously adjusted up; repeat up by half steps.

KEY WORD	FUNCTION	EXERCISE
40. placement	developing resonance within closed vowels	*Buzzy zee-oh*: Sing this exercise with an embouchered face, a small mouth opening, active and raised upper lip, and the nasal passages open; retain the buzzy sensation in the /o/ vowel (as in "so"), and sing through the final note of each small phrase; repeat up by half steps.
41. placement	creating "ring" in the voice	*The buzz hum*: Sing a buzzy hum on a descending five-note scale in C major (the hum should be placed right behind the upper teeth, with the jaw not too open); then sing the same notes on a buzzy "ng"; again on "ngaw," sending the buzzy sound into the hard palate; finally, pick up the tempo and add dotted rhythms to these pitches, using the still buzzy words "mawduh-mawduh-mawduh-mawduh-maw," moving up by half steps.
42. range extension	extending range (designed around the vowel formant series of the most natural vowels in each register)	*Female range extension; male range extension*: Alignment, breath support, and forward tone placement are all integral to this exercise; begin quietly, singing on the air, and crescendo not to but past the top note; avoid collapsing posture or support on the descending notes; sing sostenuto and make the final notes beautiful; repeat up by half steps; it works fine to have both the women and men sing this exercise at the same time, choosing the matching genre of vowels, but having them sing the vowels as written for them; use "ee-ay..." and "ah-ay..." for warming up brighter, open vowels, and use "oo-oh..." and "aw-oh..." for warming up darker, closed vowels.
43. registers	moving smoothly between the registers	*Moving between registers*: The key to this exercise is forward placement; begin with an embouchered face and with the mouth almost closed, singing *uh* through the upper teeth (this half singing–half *v* helps the voice move through the registers early in the rehearsal); sing legato almost to the point of sliding between the pitches; repeat up by half steps.

Zee - oh, zee - oh, zee - oh.

Hmm.
Ng.
Ngaw.

Maw - duh, maw - duh, maw - duh, maw - duh, maw.

S/A

Ee - ay - ah - ay - ee.
Oo - oh - aw - oh - oo.

T/B

Ah - ay - ee - ay - ah.
Aw - oh - oo - oh - aw.

(attributed to Bruce Foote)

Uh, uh, uh.

KEY WORD	FUNCTION	EXERCISE
44. registers	moving smoothly between the registers	*Moving between registers:* Because of the opening vowel sound of "oh," the lips should begin in the shape of a small circle with the lips slightly extended, much like blowing through a straw, with the jaw not too open; the placement should feel high in the dome of the hard palate, the area above the tongue; when moving from "oh" to "ee," keep the lips in that same rounded formation; slightly slide (glissando) between all pitches; add more airflow on the top pitch and less on the lower pitches; repeat up by half steps.
45. ring	developing ring through keeping the nasal passages open	*Ding-dongs:* Move from the hard, clear *d*'s immediately to the *ng*, not spending any time on the vowel; when singing the *ng*'s, continue to support and sing full; repeat up by half steps.
46. silent pulse	retaining inner pulse in interludes or long notes	*Popcorn pulse tester:* Have the singers close their eyes and make no movement or sound; the director counts aloud in a steady tempo from one to ten; the choir continues to count silently from eleven to fifty in exactly the tempo set by the director; the singers are instructed to clap one time loudly when they reach fifty (the clap comes *on* fifty); the result is a popcorn effect with a variance of up to twenty sec-onds when singers reach their own fifty; the point is to show that our inner pulses are not steady, which affects rests and longer sustained notes; use this when the choir needs a mid-rehearsal change of pace or when you are not pressed for time.

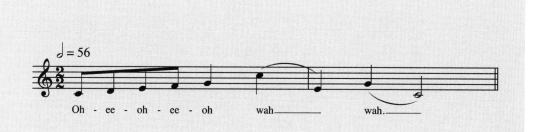

Oh - ee - oh - ee - oh   wah. _____   wah. _____

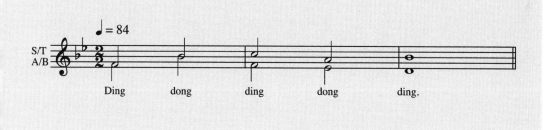

Ding   dong   ding   dong   ding.

KEY WORD	FUNCTION	EXERCISE
47. spirituals	developing characteristic color for spirituals and Russian music	*A weightier, darker sound*: On a G pitch using the numbers "1–2–3–4–5," sing four unhurried, sternum-centered quarter notes, phrased two and two, followed by a longer final note; make the following adjustments: umlaut all vowels, rounding and extending the lips to a smaller circle; modify each vowel toward the next more closed vowel— e.g., modify /ɑ/ (as in "father") toward /ɔ/ (as in "saw"), and /ɔ/ ("saw") toward /o/ (as in "so"); now sing the exercise again, sliding up slightly from just below the pitch to "1, 3, and 5"; the final word "five" will have a tinge of *oy*; now put all of these elements of sound and style into the first phrase of "sometimes I feel like a motherless child," sliding up slightly on accented (underlined) syllables; you could use this as a regular warm-up exercise by repeating this phrase up by half steps.
48. staccato	developing a lighter staccato style of articulation	*Staccato humbahs*: Each two notes is a pair in this exercise; the first word closes immediately to the *m* but is sustained into the second note, which is staccato; throw that note away with energy; clear the space before each new beat, allowing a clean entrance; repeat up by half steps.
49. staccato	alternating staccato and legato; adding energy to the rehearsal	*Legato staccato zee-ahs*: This vibrant exercise is an exceptional way to add energy to the opening of a rehearsal; the foot stomps and hand flicks are fun, but require concentration since they come at different times; the opening legato arpeggio is wonderful to sing, springing into staccatos and back to legato; obviously, the choir must be stand-ing and fully engaged; the hand flicks are not just finger motions, but powerful flinging sensations of trying to get something off of the hands; repeat up by half steps.
50. staccato	developing the flexibility to move from legato to staccato	*Numbers into hah-hahs*: The numbers should be sung portato (crisp initiations as in staccato but with the smooth follow-through of legato); the key to the descending line is keeping the breath support (and therefore the airflow) consistent on the way down; aim for the last note and sing it tenuto (its full value); avoid collapsing alignment on the descending line; repeat up by half steps.

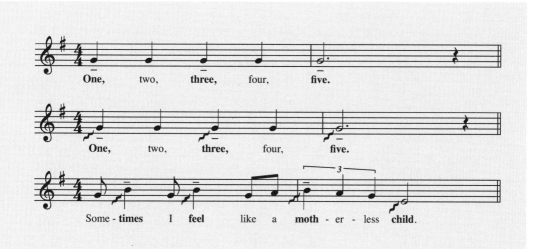

One, two, three, four, five.

One, two, three, four, five.

Some - times I feel like a moth - er - less child.

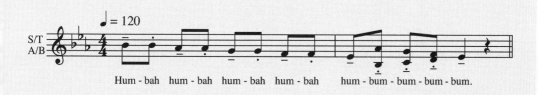

S/T
A/B

$\quad = 120$

Hum - bah hum - bah hum - bah hum - bah hum - bum - bum - bum - bum.

$\quad = 92$

* +

Zee_____ ah ah ah ah._____

* foot stomps
+ finger flicks

(attributed to the Chicago Children's Choir)

$\quad = 140$

One two three four five six sev'n eight

nine hah hah hah hah hah hah hah hah.

KEY WORD	FUNCTION	EXERCISE
51. staccato	staccato singing with phrasing contour	*Metronome canon*: These staccatos are easier to sing if you feel each measure as a phrase, with the first eighth note receiving a little linear stress, and then the next three eighth notes begin pulling toward the first beat of the next measure; eighth notes especially pull toward the longer notes, giving shape to the phrase; the breath support should be continuous, not starting and stopping for each staccato; when surrounded by staccatos, the longer notes tend to be accented and then uneven, but they should be sung smoothly with ample airflow; note that after all parts have sung the entire canon, a stopping place needs to be set, with all parts ending together on the first note of the last measure of whichever part they are on.

The Metronome

Suggestion: After all voices have sung all parts, then stop together on the first note of the last measure.

Text: Harry Robert Wilson
Text copyright © 1943 (Renewed) by Hall & McCreary Company.
International copyright secured. Printed in U.S.A. Used by permission.

Tune: Ludwig van Beethoven, 1770–1827
(Theme later used in 2nd movement of the Eighth Symphony).

Canons, Songs and Blessings: A Kemp Family Collection (CGC-27)
by Helen and John Kemp. Copyright © 1990 Choristers Guild.
All rights reserved. Printed in U.S.A. Reproduction in any portion
or form is prohibited without publisher's permission.

KEY WORD	FUNCTION	EXERCISE
52. swing	making choirs comfortable with "swing"	*Swing doh-dee-dooms*: This is a good exercise when preparaing to sing a swing or dance-oriented number; sing the dotted eighths tenuto and smoothly, feeling the ebb and flow of the rhythms; weaving, swaying, waltzing with yourself or others would free up the style; the style is sustained throughout, but not stiff; repeat up by half steps.
53. syncopation	teaching syncopated rhythms	*Syncopation canon*: Have the choir speak the numbers 1–2–3–4–5–6–7–8 in a portato style (crisp but not staccato); then again, this time noticeably accenting 1–2–<u>3</u>–4–<u>5</u>–6–<u>7</u>–8 (the typical accents in a $\frac{4}{4}$ meter); then say the numbers again accenting 1–2–3–<u>4</u>–5–6–<u>7</u>–8 (the typical syncopation in jazz), with the 4 receiving the heaviest accent in this measure; now divide the choir in half and speak the last two styles as a canon, looping from the $\frac{4}{4}$ accents to the syncopation over and over; the first half of the choir should begin with $\frac{4}{4}$, and when they move to the syncopation, the second half should begin with the $\frac{4}{4}$; there should be an obvious difference between the accented and unaccented numbers; have the choir stand and improvise body movements that match those rhythms.
54. tone color	focusing vowel sounds; enriching vocal color	*Enriching vocal color*: Sing this exercise with an open throat, good breath support, and ample airflow; repeat, having the singers cup their hands in front of their mouths like a megaphone; the echo sound they will hear will be obvious to them; then have them hold their "hand megaphones" about four inches in front of their mouths and sing again, aiming their sound into their hands and trying not to lose any of the echo quality from before; now have the singers extend their "hand megaphones" all the way out in front, still aiming their voices into their hands and still retaining the sense of echo; then drop the hands and sing again, retaining the echo quality in their voices; now repeat up by half steps.

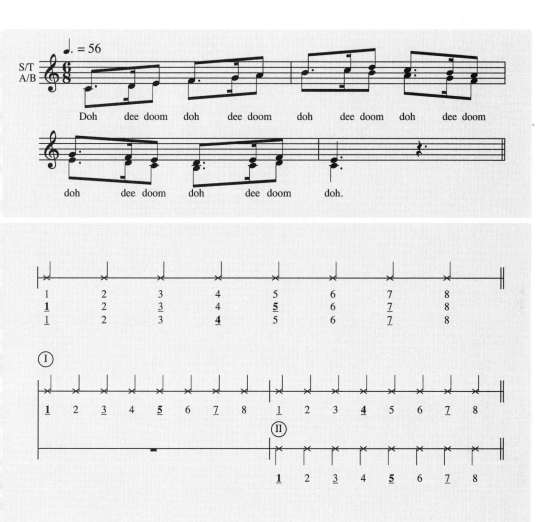

KEY WORD	FUNCTION	EXERCISE
55a. tuning	phrase momentum; tuning	*Scale into chords and variation for eight parts*: Concentrate on alignment and breath support for this exercise; the momentum and airflow must carry through and past the high note; descending scale passages are more difficult in terms of tone placement and articulation (the airflow in a descending line tends to slow, causing the placement to fall back into the throat and the notes to slide); when each part reaches its sustained note, it should diminuendo and limit vibrato for better tuning; the eight-part variation in 55b is marvelous for large choirs.

(attributed to William Trego)

KEY WORD	FUNCTION	EXERCISE
55b. tuning	phrase momentum; tuning	See 55a.

KEY WORD	FUNCTION	EXERCISE
56. tuning	adjusting major thirds	*Major or minor thirds and variations revoiced and in four parts*: These exercises are built to teach the concept that the major third in a typical chord needs to be adjusted slightly upward to tune well; in the first chord, the sopranos and altos have the third and need to adjust up; when their pitch changes, the tenors are on the third of the chord, and they need to adjust, and so forth; in the second variation, the men are often on the third, which is excellent for bass sections who tend to flat; the four-part variation adds more complexity and is quite lovely; continue alternately moving down by half steps until out of easy register.
57. tuning	adjusting major thirds	*Adding thirds to open fifths*: Have the accompanist play a variety of open fifths, to which the choir, on signal from the conductor, adds the major third of the chord, always adjusting up; caution your leaders to not be aggressive, loud, or early, allowing all choir members to work at finding the pitch.
58. tuning	alternating unisons and chords	*Chords for tuning*: Tuning unisons time and time again after briefly singing other notes is a great challenge; this exercise begins simply in unison, then divides into two parts, and then into four; emphasize the tuning of the unisons more than the chords; it's a more difficult skill; repeat up by half steps.

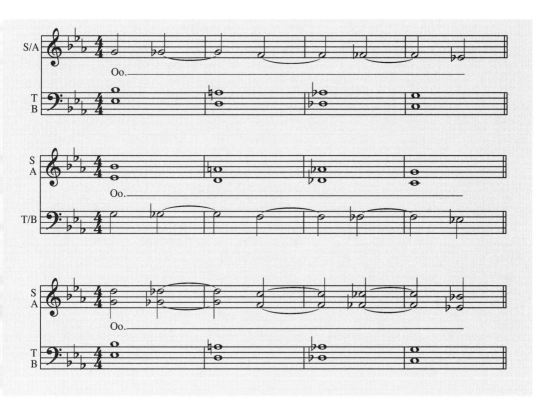

(attributed to Lara Haggard)

KEY WORD	FUNCTION	EXERCISE
59a. tuning chords	listening to and tuning changing chords	*Do-re-mi's in three parts with two variations, plus a four-part variation*: In exercises 59a–c, the complexity is not in the pitches sung, because they never change for anyone; the pitches and the syllables are invariable, but the order and timing of entrances creates varying inversions and chords, and each section's position in the chords in constantly changing; the sound of the chords is beautiful to be in the middle of; the four-part variation in 59d has parallel thirds on the outsides, with parallel seconds on the inside; partly consonant, partly dissonant; it is an effective way to become comfortable with dissonance.

(attributed to Lloyd Pfautsch)

KEY WORD	FUNCTION	EXERCISE
59b. tuning chords	listening to and tuning changing chords	See 59a.

KEY WORD	FUNCTION	EXERCISE
59c. **tuning chords**	listening to and tuning changing chords	See 59a.

KEY WORD	FUNCTION	EXERCISE
59d. **tuning chords**	listening to and tuning changing chords	See 59a.

KEY WORD	FUNCTION	EXERCISE
60. vocal	vocal exuberance; rhythmic ensemble	*Yup canon*: The opening staccatos need to be moderately quiet but sternum–centered, with an upward feeling; make sure of the accuracy of the pitches on the main beats of measure 2; the third measure on should be aggressive, fun singing; the final "hey" should be a real full-throated but staccato shout; once learned in unison, sing as a canon of up to four parts, with new parts entering at each measure.
61. vocal	vocal exuberance; singing descending lines	*Descending scale fah-lah-lahs*: This exercise uses full-throated singing; since descending lines tend to lose focus and airflow, first sing an ascending scale with the same rhythms as listed; then retain that feeling and sing the music as written (when you sing down a scale, use the support and articulation you would use if singing up); repeat up by half steps.
62. vocal color	tone color differences between women and men	*Gender Vowel-Color Differences*: At the same time, have the women or girls sing the pitches 8–7–6–5–5–6–7–8 on an /u/ vowel (as in "soon") while the men or boys sing the pitches 8–7–6–5–4–3–2–1 on an /ɔ/ vowel (as in "saw"); begin in B♭ major and move up by half steps; because of the natural characteristics of their voices in the part of the voice that they use the most, women and girls need to generally close their vowels more than the men, and this exercise trains that habit.

Yup,* yup, yup, yup, yup dee yup dee yup dee aye. Tra -
la la la la la la la la la la la la, tra - la la la, tra - la! Hey!

* yup = rhymes with foot.

Text and Tune: Christian Lahusen
from Kanonbüchlein, BA1221
Copyright © Bärenreiter-Verlag, Kassel & Basel. Used by permission.

Fah lah lah lah lah lah lah,

pah pah pah pah pah pah pah pah.

Oo.

Aw.

CHAPTER 13

CONDUCTOR CONCERNS REGARDING REHEARSALS

OVERVIEW

The following concerns were gathered from choral conductors around the country, along with those regarding the voice found earlier in the book. They represent the kind of frustrations that get in the way of effective and enjoyable rehearsals. For the most part, they are not scholarly questions, but it is often these practical problems that keep us from enjoying our jobs and getting the most out of our rehearsals. Most are people-oriented concerns that clearly require sensitivity, psychology, and a good bit of common sense. As is so often true, people are at the center of what we do, and we cannot achieve aesthetic success without learning to work well with people and learning to be creative in solving problems. Artists have to remember to live gracefully in the real world.

CONDUCTOR CONCERNS AND SOLUTIONS

How to begin rehearsals when the choir comes in hyper.

When the choir arrives for rehearsal, quickly assess their mood and adjust your style and demeanor to counterbalance their mood. If they come in animated, playful and full of pep, you should counter with poise, speaking intentionally lower, slower, and quieter. Avoid being drawn into casual conversations, which signals others to continue theirs. Use smaller conducting gestures to focus their attention. Choose a warm-up that is sustained and calm, working on tuning and other more subtle skills. Do the exercise seated.

How to begin rehearsals when the choir comes in lethargic.

If the choir comes in dragging and listless, counter by being much more upbeat, going out of your way to greet individuals and make them feel welcome. Your speech should be more animated, slightly higher in pitch, intensity, and volume. Your gestures should now be larger and more dramatic. Choose a warm-up built on full singing, staccatos, accents, and playfulness. Get the choir standing and include kinesthetic movements to make the exercise more fun.

An accompanist who is always just ahead of or behind the conductor's beat.

In front of the accompanist, explain to the choir that the better musicians they become, the more accurately they will be able to follow the subtle nuances of the conductor's beat. Before you have them work on this, you want to show them what it means to be able to follow exactly. Explain that you are going to conduct the accompanist for a few measures of the next anthem, making small changes in the tempo and even holding certain chords. Tell them to aware of how well the accompanist is following your conducting, because they are next. By this time, the accompanist's reputation is on the line, and he or she will be right with you. Then repeat the exercise having the choir clap eighth notes while the accompanist continues to play, everyone following the small changes of tempo of the conductor. Then have the choir clap as the tempo changes without the help of the accompanist. Make a big thing of thanking the accompanist for his or her precision. The point has been well made.

One additional thought: When the accompaniment is not precisely with you, ask that the accompanist play for a moment without using the damper pedal at all, which sometimes covers up a world of sin.

Strong singers who sing behind the beat.

Have the choir sing a few passages using very short staccatos. Strong singers love to sing legato, because they can sing louder and others notice their leadership. Short staccatos cannot be sung loudly. Describe the staccatos you want as lifting rebounds. Then have half of the choir continue to sing the staccatos, but the other half sing legato . . . quietly enough to still hear the crispness of the staccatos. The legato half will almost always be late. Make them aware of that, repeat the exercise, and then switch roles. Even the strong, normally late singers get lined up.

Lack of retention from one rehearsal to the next.

Make a point of summarizing what was accomplished on each piece of music before moving on to another piece. What section of the music had the hardest notes? Did they mark their music in some way that would help them not make those mistakes again? What choral or vocal skills did it take to make the music sound good? What section of the music will you work hardest on next time? This type of short wrap-up helps choir members remember this week's accomplishments when they take out the music again at the next rehearsal or in a coming performance. Conductors already know this. Singers' retention would improve if that information were shared.

Reviewing performances with choirs.

Reviewing performances with your choir can be tricky. The choir has worked hard for weeks, culminating in a performance. Good or bad, that performance is over, and nothing further can be done to fix problems. Candidly ripping choir members about where they fell short makes them feel bad about themselves without any opportunity to do anything about it. Choir members do, however, inevitably want to know what you thought. There is no need to tell them everything you think. You can always find good and bad things about any performance, so choose two or three good things to compliment them on. Then add no more than one suggestion for growth, one skill that needs to come up to the level of the other compliments you listed. Ask the choir to take that one skill on as a special goal for the next performance, but end by thanking them for their hard work. Regarding playing recordings of your performances, only do this occasionally when a small segment of some performance went about as well as your choir has ever sung. Play just that for the choir, and get back to work renewed, refreshed, reassured.

Making the best use of rehearsal time when all of the decent readers in a section are absent.

All conductors hate those rehearsals. Notes that have never been a concern for that voice part are suddenly nowhere near secure. You find yourself distracted, tediously going over and over the same notes for the same section, spending eighty percent of the rehearsal on one voice part while the other three sections get frustrated. It is counterproductive, and, frankly, it is naïve to think that those singers can ever sing confidently without their leaders.

I take a different tack. If you know that those absent leaders are reliable and prepared, then back off. Don't fret unduly about that voice part this rehearsal, and don't invest inordinate time drilling their notes. If you are concerned, call an extra sectional rehearsal that the leaders can also attend. But in the main rehearsal, start concentrating on the voice parts that are capable right now of moving fast and making significant progress. Let the other section without leadership sing along as well as they can, but get off their backs. When the leaders are back, they will be okay, but for now you have much else to accomplish and much more music to learn.

Achieving effective proportions between the voice parts.

As a part of your score study, decide which voice parts should be dominant. Perhaps, as in a hymn, the melody is in the soprano or the tenor, and the other voice parts harmonize. But often the thematic material jumps from voice part to voice part. In your conductor's score, draw angled arrows leading your eye from one predominant part to another. Have the choir underline the text whenever their section has the theme (although the theme is not primarily about the text, this method of marking seems more practical than circling the notes). To make sure the singers are clear about where these themes occur and their responsibility to emphasize them, have each section stand when it sings the theme, sitting as soon as the theme moves to another section. Now sing the music again; this time, rather than having those with the theme stand, have them sing the text while the other accompanying voices sing *oo*. Explain afterwards that this is the balance that you would like to effect: when all parts are singing the text, *accompanying* voices must sing a dynamic level less than marked, and *theme* singers need to increase their level slightly. Also explain that if the theme lies lower in a section's vocal range, the dynamic level will need to be even higher to project over the accompanying voices. In your conducting, be obvious about giving those with the theme most of your attention.

When and how often to use staggered breathing.

The intention of staggered breathing has always been to better serve the text. If you would not breathe in a certain place when speaking the text, it seems self-evident that it would be better for the singers not to breathe there either, using instead staggered breathing. Staggered breathing produces a lovely, serene effect reminiscent of the sustained eloquence of a pipe organ. There are, however, some drawbacks to its overuse. Music such as church hymns and folk songs that were originally intended for the community to sing, as opposed to trained choirs, must have been envisioned with regular breathing places, regardless of the text. If a choir is helping to lead or imitating community singing of such music, they should probably also breathe when practical, rather than when text appropriate. Another concern with staggered breathing has to do with the natural arsis and thesis, or ebb and flow, of the musical phrases. Staggered breathing significantly limits the contouring of phrases. When a breath is taken, it gives the phrase a place to gradually let down, to rest, which adds dramatically to the effect of the growth of the next phrase. This happens naturally with the upbows and downbows of string music. When staggered breathing is employed, the phrases never really relax, and the ear is not drawn with anticipation to the next phrase. So use staggered breathing with discretion, keeping an ear out for the musical effect. When you do use it, use text emphasis to still create a sense of arsis and thesis.

Retaining energy in quiet, sustained music.
Energy dissipates when singers sing from note to note instead of singing phrases. Warm up with long, slow crescendos and diminuendos, making sure that spinal alignment is healthy and that the airflow is steady under the voice. Then using a selection of music to be rehearsed, target the high points of long notes or phrases at specific places further down the musical line. Begin phrases quieter than normal, almost growing from nothing. Keep aiming toward those high points with the same, slow, controlled crescendos with which you warmed up. Once there, allow the phrase to relax gradually, before beginning the next crescendo. Diminuendos are much more difficult than crescendos because of the tendency to inadvertently use less air, causing the tone placement to get throaty and the efficiency of the vocal production to suffer. In diminuendos, concentrate on using ample air. Long, quiet phrases are also enhanced by the kinesthetic device of having the singers point a forefinger ahead of them while singing the phrase. Starting waist high, they should gradually move the finger forward and up until the phrase is finished. This helps sustain a vitality throughout the phrase.

Teaching choirs to stress important words and convey moods.
Every once in a while, have your choir read the text of the music (typed out by itself) before rehearsing it. Ask them what its mood is, and after some discussion, have them write in that mood at the top of the first page of music. Then have the choir read the text again, circling the most descriptive words, the words that give the most significant meaning to the text. Lastly, have them circle the same words in their voice parts of the music. Urge the choir to sing with understanding, endeavoring to convey the emotions of the text as they sing. After singing through with this emphasis, ask if they felt their body language and visage matched the mood they were conveying with their voices. Urge them to be actors and actresses, advocates for the text in every way they can. In subsequent pieces of music, including multiple movements of major works in Latin, dictate to them the moods they should write in their music at the beginning of each piece or movement. Make a difference between the moods of those movements. Don't let them be soulless singers.

CHAPTER 14

ADDITIONAL IDEAS FOR ENERGIZING REHEARSALS

Rehearsals need energy to be effective, and that energy can be stimulated by creating a sense of intrigue, which fires the imaginations of the singers, something that is different from the routine. There should be some unexpected variety in every rehearsal, whether it is in the room setup, the seating order, or the way each piece of music is approached. This chapter presents some additional ideas for enlivening your rehearsals. Read through them and find a couple that seem like they would work for you and your choir, adapting the ideas as needed. The main point is to continually strive to make each rehearsal fresh. Use these ideas to get started and then follow your imagination!

1. Use two alternating seating charts for rehearsals. The first is the basic performance order with four separate sections. The second is for double choir, placing half of the choir on one side and the other half on the other side. If your choir rehearses multiple times a week, perhaps this alternate double-choir seating could be used for the final rehearsal each week. If you have one rehearsal a week, use the double-choir seating every third rehearsal. In the double-choir seating order, make sure that the sight-reading and vocal leadership for each section is evenly divided. When the double-choir order is used, have the two half choirs compete with one another, singing phrases back and forth and comparing sound and accuracy.

2. If you have the talent and instruments available, consider using two pianos to speed note-learning, one for playing the choral parts and the other for the accompaniment. This is particularly beneficial when rehearsing more complex music, such as movements from major choral-orchestral works.

3. Put enough physical space between the singers' chairs to allow for freedom of sound and movement, and a sense of

the importance of individual effort, focus, and musical independence.

4. Rather than listing the order of music to be rehearsed on the board, add an element of intrigue and curiosity to the moment by giving hints about the music to be rehearsed next. Ask the choir to take out the piece in E♭ major, or the one in $\frac{6}{8}$ meter, or the one that has an ABA form, or the music that tells an Old Testament story. This gets the singers to look intellectually through the music for clues, a quick change of pace before starting in on a new piece.

5. The process of working on each piece of music in rehearsal should be approached the same way a novelist writes a new chapter in a book. Each approach should be a little different for each piece of music to be rehearsed, capturing the singers' imaginations and sustaining their interest. Rehearsals have two goals: to teach the notes and to continually build choral skills. Regarding the second, each piece of music contains many such opportunities for teaching. By judiciously choosing different mini-goals for each piece of music, your rehearsals retain freshness and vitality.

6. Where is your attention during rehearsal? There are substantial benefits to looking up from your music more often, such as maintaining eye contact with choir members (which forces them to watch you more closely), evaluating their mood, checking their posture, noticing if they are marking your instructions or their own note concerns as they go, and judging when it would be best to move on to another piece of music. When you as the conductor find yourself reading each note as you go, you are less aware of how closely the choir is reacting to your conducting gestures. You also are not able to evaluate matters of tuning, blend, tone color, proportion, rhythmic ensemble, style of articulation, diction, and mood. Analyzing the form of the music makes it possible to look up more often. For example, a common form might be a 4-measure piano introduction, an 8-measure choral phrase (A), a contrasting 8-measure phrase (B), a 2-measure interlude, a repeat of the 8-measure A phrase, and another 8-measure phrase that begins like B, but has a different ending (B′). Your score study has indicated that the only anticipated note problems are in phrases B and B′, so you are free to look up at your singers while counting measures mentally until you approach the B areas of more obvious note concern. Of course, you can always look down to refresh yourself or if concerns arise, but the feeling that you are communicating back and forth with the choir has

been set. The point is that your knowledge of the form will enable you to look up more often and be a more sensitive evaluator of your singers and their sound.

7. When learning pitches, have all the sections sing the voice part of the weakest sight-reading section. Then, while two sections sing that same part again, have the strongest sight-reading section join the next weakest section on that voice part. Next, have the two weakest sections sing their notes without the help of the stronger sections. Finally, add the stronger sections singing their own parts. The advantage of this process is that the weaker sight-reading sections have twice the run-throughs and twice the help learning their notes, and the stronger sight-reading sections enjoy the challenge of reading the other parts.

8. Earlier in the process of learning new music, consider having the choir speak (not sing) the rhythm of their own voice parts using Kodaly-oriented rhythmic nomenclature—e.g., *ta* for a quarter note, *ti* for an eighth note, *tie* for a dotted note, and *toe* for a longer note. (Even Kodaly experts do not agree about the specific terms, so use what is most comfortable for you.) Have half of the choir repeat this while the other half speaks the text. Then switch assignments.

9. Take a page from Robert Shaw and occasionally use count-singing instead of text or *lah-lahs*, meaning the choir sings numbers on every eighth-note value—e.g., "one and two and three and four"—on their correct pitches. The problem is that many choir directors try to use this rhythmic ensemble device when first learning a piece of music. It is not usually helpful as an aid to the initial learning of music. For those of us who have unauditioned choirs with a wide variety of musical experience and inexperience, we have to keep in mind that many volunteer singers keep their places by following the text, and therefore count-singing early in the learning process is frustrating and even counter-productive. If the purpose of count-singing is to build rhythmic ensemble, then it will be more effective after the basic notes are learned. When teaching the concept and coordination of count-singing for the first time, choose a simple, less challenging passage to get the choir used to the idea. When the choir's comfort level grows, have one half of the choir sing the text and the other half count-sing, and then switch assignments.

10. Add variety and energy to rehearsals through kinesthetic teaching, using movements of various kinds to underscore certain stylistic ideas and facilitate learning—e.g., fists hitting palms on major beats to gain a more vibrant vitality, fingers flashing open in front of the face on accents, hand motions to follow the contour of a phrase, the edges of fingers placed along the upper jaw as a reminder of forward tone placement, swaying to capture a feeling of dance, marching in marcato phrases.

11. The dominant points in a melody are often a long note after a short one, the first of two repeated notes, the last note before a change of direction, or the note assigned to an important syllable of the text. For developing more natural flow in a musical phrase, determine these dominant points of linear stress in the phrase, and then sing a legato *dah* on those notes, and a portato (halfway between legato and staccato) *doot* on all other notes. The nonstressed notes are called *arsic* (lifting or leading toward), and the dominant notes are called *thetic* (the culminating point of stress). After dictating where the *dah*s are to be placed in the first few phrases and when the choir seems comfortable with this procedure, have them make up their own *dah*s and *doot*s for a few passages, each choir member intuiting where to use each word, acknowledging that there will not be complete agreement. The point is to develop a sense of ebb and flow, of rise and fall, of arsis and thesis, in the choir's singing. Then start again, this time having half the choir sing the *dah*s and *doot*s while the other half sings the text quietly, but matching the natural ebb and flow of the *dah*s and *doot*s. Then switch roles. Finally, have the whole choir sing the text being sensitive to the natural rise and fall of the phrases.

12. Be wary of pontificating. Be philosophical, explain texts, and give historical background just enough to add depth and understanding to the choir's singing. Sharing too much of such knowledge may be perceived as "look how much I know" instead of adding to the choral experience. So keep a balance between the efficiency of note-learning and just enough philosophical depth to keep choir members motivated and informed. If what you are about to say slows down note-learning without substantially enhancing the choral experience, don't say it. Be particularly aware of being drawn into pontificating after attending choral workshops.

13. See chapter 23, "Keeping Rehearsals Alive."

CHAPTER 15

WHAT IS DIFFERENT ABOUT CONDUCTING INSTRUMENTALISTS?

OVERVIEW

I have been fortunate enough to have my own full orchestras for the past seventeen years, conducting some three hundred works of the standard repertoire. Choral conductors who hire occasional instrumentalists or a large orchestra for a major work need to think differently when preparing for those rehearsals. As a professional violist myself, I offer these insights into the mindset of instrumentalists and suggestions on how to work most effectively with them.

THE DIFFERENCES BETWEEN SINGERS AND INSTRUMENTALISTS

- Instrumentalists have to learn much more music with far less rehearsal than choruses.
- Because of the complexity of their parts and always-limited rehearsal time, instrumentalists depend heavily on a conductor's knowledge of the score and clear gestures.
- Instrumentalists do not respond to "pep talks," emotional explanations, or philosophical lectures about the meaning of the music. They are only concerned with rehearsals that help them to play well and feel safe.
- Aside from the strings, all orchestral players are the only ones on their part, which means they are always exposed and feel a strong sense of individual responsibility.
- In an orchestra, there is no expert pianist to help players learn their notes or to cover their problems if they lose their place.

TYPICAL FRUSTRATIONS OF ORCHESTRAL PLAYERS

- Choral conductors who ignore the orchestra, giving their attention primarily to the choir with whom they rehearse every week.
- Conductors who don't know the orchestral score, and therefore don't give important cues.
- Conductors with unclear gestures or who do not use traditional patterns.
- Conductors whose tempos are erratic.
- Conductors who take unrealistically fast tempos learned from recordings of top professional orchestras with much more rehearsal time.
- Conductors who show a lack of respect for the musicianship of the instrumentalists.

EXPECTATIONS ORCHESTRAL PLAYERS HAVE OF CONDUCTORS

- Always give "safety" cues for entrances when an instrumentalist has been idle for a matter of measures, especially timpani and percussion players.
- Rehearse quickly and efficiently with a minimum of needless talking.
- Listen for such details as balance and give clear instructions.
- Make corrections or suggestions concisely and accurately and get right back to the music.
- Use exact Italian terms rather than lengthy explanations about what the music should feel like.
- Give anacruses (pickups) in the same tempo as the coming music.
- In ritards at the end of movements, conduct the most active part, usually the timpani.
- Between movements, look up to see if all the instrumentalists are ready. They may have awkward page turns, or possibly even need to change instruments between movements (e.g., clarinets or oboes/English horns).
- For dangerous entrances, ask if the orchestra would prefer two beats "for free" (preparatory beats), but don't conduct a whole measure for free.
- Unless the conductor is a string player, trust the concertmaster to make bowing decisions, but get him or her the music well in advance.

STRATEGIES FOR REHEARSING AN ORCHESTRA

- Describe or model the type of phrase contour you desire for thematic material (e.g., where the high point of the phrase should be).
- Be aware of how much bow the strings are using. If the notes are fast and the string sound is not clear, ask them to use less bow and play slightly closer to the bridge.
- Become conversant with the most common styles of bowing (e.g., hooked bowing). If you would prefer to have a section played more staccato with shorter notes, say so. Follow your musical instincts. If you don't like the sound you hear, ask the concertmaster for advice on how to achieve the sound you desire.
- Always be aware of proportions, not only between the orchestra and chorus, but also between the various parts of the orchestra. In the beginning of the Mozart *Requiem*, for example, the long, slow solo lines of the bassoons and clarinets are often covered up by the overdone eighth notes of the strings.
- In fugal passages, ask that whoever has the theme to play up a dynamic level, and those who don't to play a level quieter.
- Listen for the quality of pizzicato, and if it is not clear, ask that the string players make a better connection with the string to brighten up that sound. The sound of pizzicatos is often lost completely because the players' fingers are brushing against the strings instead of making a strong contact.

PART III

MOTIVATING FOR SUCCESS

INTRODUCTION

If you were a violinist and you had a good instrument, the quality of your efforts would be a simple matter of your personal hard work, talent, and education. As a choir director, on the other hand, attaining quality results is a much more complex task, because our instrument is the choir. Unlike a violin, choir members have personalities that can either enhance or hinder rehearsals and performances. When things are going well—that is, choir members are in the mood to sing, highly energized, well focused, friendly, supportive, and yearning to learn—then directing the group is a pleasure and the results are productive. But as often as not, the choir you face at the beginning of rehearsal is anything but focused. Body language shows signs of apathy and perhaps strain, faces are placid, souls are uninspired. Unless you do something to lift choir members' spirits with a vision of self-worth, beauty, and higher purpose, the chances of making exceptional music with and through the choir are slim to none.

The good news is that finding yourself in front of a listless choir does not mean that you write that rehearsal off as hopelessly unproductive. You can turn your choir members' low energy around with creativity and unstoppable optimism that can make every moment of the rehearsal productive and alive. We all have the choice between optimism and pessimism. Most singers don't make a conscious decision about which way to be or feel on any given day. They just find themselves there in your rehearsals, sometimes inexplicably scattered or sluggish. Not to worry. With a little creative sensitivity, you can usually do something to help their mood . . . and therefore your rehearsal.

Here are ideas for motivating your choirs, which should result in heightened commitment, regularity of attendance, the desire to improve, team building within the choir, the willingness to study music outside of rehearsals, and an overall buoyant and progressive spirit. These basic concepts come from people professionals: psychologists and salesmen, business executives and coaches, conductors, teachers, and ministers. These thought-provoking ideas are grouped logically by their specific uses. They begin with ways conductors can help motivate themselves—as always, the first step to motivating others. You will learn to see everything about rehearsing from the perspective of the singers—what's it like to be a singer in your choir? There are aspects of your planning process that effect motivation; so do the looks of the rehearsal room. There are helpful ideas for how you work more sensitively with your choir members, using psychology to create a positive environment. We can all use help dealing with those sensitive people-problems that so often seem to take the air out of our sails, creating unnecessary animosity and touchy feelings—certainly impediments to a successful choir program. So use these ideas to fill your sails with fresh air, and lift your choir to new levels of enjoyment and productivity.

CHAPTER 16

GET YOURSELF MOTIVATED FIRST

ENTHUSIASM

Let the image of your personal enthusiasm and deeply felt convictions impact the morale of the choir from the second you walk in the room. Constantly be aware of your facial expressions and body language. Are you encouraging and happy, or do you slip unknowingly into frowns and severity? Cheer on the choir all the time! Never let down. Be so completely engaged and enthusiastic in your rehearsals that your choir members feel that they are the only choir in the world and that you would rather be there with them than with any other choir. They perceive the mood without your ever saying a word and leave each rehearsal refreshed and eager to come the next time. Work with what you have rather than wishing you were with a better choir. With a great attitude from you, they can and will improve.

MAKE YOUR MOOD CHOICE

Happiness is not something you have to figure out how to achieve. You don't have to search it out, nor do something extraordinary to deserve it. It's a choice. You can either decide to be happy or unhappy. Whatever mood you choose as your default attitude compounds itself as you move through your day. If you carry around a sour mood, your choirs and your colleagues will send the same dismal mood back your way. On the other hand, you can simply make a decision to be happy, to smile at people and genuinely care about them, to lose yourself in others, to be resilient and handle life's bumps with courage and optimism, grateful to be doing such a positive thing with your life. Check out your choir; they are most likely sending back to you what they are getting from you. If you don't like what you see, fix yourself first! Your mood is as much your responsibility as is the accuracy and musicality of the music. Without a positive spirit in the choir, all your academic and scholarly knowledge is worthless.

GET IN THE MOOD BY PLAYING THE PART

Conductors are performers. Sometimes we have to get beyond our own mood of the moment in order to lead our singers effectively. So back up and use the skills of a performer before rehearsal even begins. If you don't happen to be in a buoyant mood that day, be a great actor. Look the part; feel the part. Soon your buoyancy is making singers smile, and that helps *you* smile! Our job is to be proactive in mood setting. Don't walk into that rehearsal room without caring enough to bring a good mood along with you!

CARING

Let people see how much you care. Make it obvious to your choir that how they feel and how they sing are enormously important to you. Let rehearsals be more than cerebral affairs. The choir needs to feel your emotions as their inspirational foundation.

THE POWER OF A SMILE

Welcome your choir with a genuine smile. Lift that upper lip a little. Let your eyes be bright and open. Raise your cheeks (sometimes called flaring the nostrils). Just before each rehearsal, take a look in the mirror and get that smile on your face and warmth in your demeanor. Then go on into the rehearsal room to spread the good feelings to others. Your smile can lift the mood of your whole choir.

THE SMILE ROUTINE

I have a simple routine that I follow to make sure I always have a smile on my face before rehearsals. I put a fist about six inches in front of my face, knuckles facing me, and fling my fingers wide open. As the fingers spring up, so does my smile! It is a simple kinesthetic reminder to me to get my face up and my smile on. It makes the choir members feel better and me, too!

HOW FRIENDLY ARE YOU?

Your success as a conductor is largely based upon choir members' reactions to how you present yourself—e.g., the warmth of your face, your eye contact, your body language, the tone quality of your voice, the inflection and pace of your speaking voice, your ability to empathize with others, the relevance of what you say and what you have to offer, your expertise, the genuineness of your care for others, and your dedication to higher goals. If we want success, we need to do the things that make us more appealing. How friendly are you? A conductor's basic friendliness can make relationships with choir members easier to form, or, on the other hand, tedious and testy. Most of us are oblivious to how we are being perceived, but we can take steps to build friendliness skills.

NOT JUST THE STARS

Just a reminder: Make sure that you are equally friendly to all members of the choir, not just the "stars." Everyone in the choir makes a contribution, and the lesser lights need motivation, perhaps more than the stars.

THE WELCOMING EFFECT

Most of the welcoming effect of your image is made visually—e.g., your uplifted face, vibrant eyes, head position and posture, and your on-the-balls-of-your-feet energy. The tone, inflection, and pace of your speaking voice give the next strongest effect. Record your speaking voice; listen to see if it has the natural musicality, tone quality, and inflection that is pleasant to listen to.

NOTICE EXPRESSIVITY

As a way to build your own skills, notice expressivity (or the lack of it) in faces you see. Rent a good movie or record a soap opera and play it back without sound. See if you can capture the intended emotions from simply watching the actors' faces. Try those expressions out on your own face and get into the habit of letting your face be more active.

CHAPTER 17

THE DISCIPLINE OF THE CONDUCTOR

THE CONDUCTOR'S SPEAKING VOICE

Keep honing your speaking voice. Have you ever heard your own speaking voice in a rehearsal? Does it model good vocal quality for your singers? Does it have enough richness and variance of inflection to create a feeling of vitality, warmth, and caring? Is your enunciation clear? Is your posture and head position conducive to natural breath support and sustained energy through a sentence or thought? Is your voice jammed by a head position that is always looking down? Is your pacing a bit too fast, leaving your choir frenetic and nervous; or too slow, losing the choir's attention and sapping the energy in the room? Is the pitch level of your voice comfortable, too low (sounding artificial) or too high (sounding pinched and weak)? Are you using good placement in your speech, meaning a balance between brightness and warmth, between clarity and emotion, between carrying power and support? Is your face (your articulators, i.e., your lips, tongue, cheeks, nostrils) active or placid? If you feel you need to know more about this, spend several sessions with a speech therapist or, perhaps, an acting coach.

THE CONDUCTOR'S EYE CONTACT

Your eye contact with your singers makes a huge impact on their energy level and concentration. Develop the habit of really looking at them when you give instructions. Make sure your gaze gradually takes in all of your singers, much like a good performer who makes each person in the audience feel personally connected. To accomplish this, occasionally conduct without looking at your music. A quick analysis of the music often reveals a logical form, which makes it possible for a conductor to look up for several measures at a time, as long as things are going well. For instance, there may be a 4-measure introduction, followed by two 8-measure phrases. Try to get through most of that segment without staring at the music, allowing you to instead concentrate on hooking your singers' attention—and on listening more carefully to how they are singing.

The Conductor's Stance and Gestures

Check out the size of your conducting gestures. Most of these need to be smaller and clearer. Exert some downward isometric weight in the heels of your hands, with rebounds coming slightly back toward your body. Feel strength in your little fingers (pinkies) and drive energy through them to the singers. This keeps the fingers from rolling into a ball, losing buoyancy in hand motions. Your upper chest carriage empathetically encourages better posture in the singers, a tall buoyancy without undo tension. As the Alexander Technique explains, there is no set good posture for a conductor, but rather a sense of perpetual lengthening (see chapter 2 on singers' posture), with a good connection between the floor and your heels. Standing on the balls of your feet creates tension and imbalance. There should be a solid, balanced floor connection between both edges of your feet and your heels. Your stance should be one of physical connection and anticipation. Everything about you should give an empathetic boost to your singers.

The Conductor's Confidence

Ever have trouble with your nerves? The solution is to be less selfish; think more about your audience or congregation than you do about yourself. Being nervous means that you are thinking about yourself: What will they think about you? Try this instead. Look at your performance as a gift you are presenting to those who are listening—even judges in a contest. What they think of the performance or you is not your concern. If they like it, that's a nice extra, but the joy is in making the music and sharing it in performance. Mind your own business, not theirs. This, by the way, works for you as conductor, for your choir members, and for individual singers preparing for solos.

The Conductor's Personal Discipline

Make use of daily rituals to keep your life and your rehearsals on a steadier path toward excellence. Get into better physical shape by setting up an exercise regimen at least three times a week. Do the same with your voice, perhaps starting each day with posture, breathing, and tongue exercises, followed by some lip trills and light vocalizing. If at all possible, schedule fifteen to twenty minutes of focus time before every rehearsal warming up your voice, putting your music in order, reviewing the opening warm-ups, and preparing your psyche to be uplifting, calm, and well paced. These daily rituals are the protective coating around your day. They keep you steady.

PROTECT YOUR DAY

Be in charge of your day. You can either make something special of it, or you can let other people and circumstances take charge, leaving you to spend the day reacting to outside influences. Think about your big goals, about what is really important to you, and, no matter what comes your way, keep taking little steps in that direction. Don't let anything or anyone get you down. Don't get dragged down into negativism. Turn everything in a positive direction. Exude confidence and caring, and fill the canvas of each day of your life with the painting you want instead of someone else's dribbles.

CHAPTER 18

MOTIVATIONAL ASPECTS OF REHEARSING

PACE THE REHEARSAL

While rehearsing a piece, avoid stopping every time you hear a mistake. Let your choir sing for a bit while you listen carefully, and then choose one or two concerns to work on. The object is to give out a few ideas choir members can assimilate, and then get right back to singing. You will have heard more problems than those one or two, of course, but choir members can only handle so much information before they become overloaded and discouraged. When you realize you have been stopping a lot and you sense growing frustration in the choir, put a ten-dollar bill on the music stand, which you promise to give to them if you stop the next time without getting all the way through! They become intrigued with the possibility that you will forget and accidentally stop, and their mood and focus grows. You will find that you must also increase your discipline to keep going, and you begin to see the piece as a whole. This approach adds some badly needed humor and keeps you on track.

USE REHEARSAL TIME WISELY

Having enough rehearsal time is always a concern. Our tendency is to be somewhat relaxed and inefficient early in rehearsals or in the early stages of learning a major work. Then, inevitably, comes the ulcerated moment when we suddenly realize how much there is left to learn in too little time. So before you begin to rehearse each piece of music, remind your choir members how many rehearsals are left for that piece. If you routinely put the rehearsal agenda on the board (or send it out in advance by e-mail), put the rehearsals remaining in parentheses beside each title. For major works, indicate how many rehearsals remain before the dress rehearsal. Diligent, careful work early on avoids the need for those frustrating rehearsal extensions and exhausting extra rehearsals.

Create Warmth through Rehearsal Breaks

Take a short break during each rehearsal. Besides relaxing the tension of sustained concentration, breaks give choir members a chance to get closer to one another, create a choir that wants to be together. Breaks help create a sense of family, a sense that we are there for one another. If the rehearsal is rather short, it might be only a 2-minute break in the action. For a longer rehearsal of up to two hours, perhaps the break could be as much as eight minutes, but not too much more than that. A good choir has too much to do, and the best of your singers come to sing, not to chat. Serving refreshments during breaks takes too much time generally, but it's not a bad idea once in a while as a special treat. For high school choirs, if you think this idea fits you, consider purchasing a tug-of-war rope for "quick breaks," when momentum has slowed and students are sluggish. A quick sopranos-vs.-altos tug-of-war, followed by the boys taking on the winner, does wonders for the energy in the room, and you can go right back to work. Use this when you need more energy, not when you need more focus.

Trust Your Instincts

Believe in your own instincts. Not all good ideas come from books or clinicians. Let yourself think and feel with a sense of instinctive artistry. Play with musical ideas of interpretation. Dream up ways to make voices sound better. Believe in your own innate musicality. Be aware of how your choir members are reacting during rehearsals and play to them like an actor plays to an audience. Such spontaneity in the act of rehearsing doesn't mean you prepare any less diligently, but don't let your preset plans stifle your imagination. Give your artistic spirit and common sense the opportunity to put a little extra zing in your rehearsals.

Make a Difference in People's Lives

As choir directors, every rehearsal brings us the opportunity to make a positive impact in people's lives. Everything we say, every moment of each rehearsal, every note we write or call we make to choir members is a significant gem of opportunity to make an impact. How do we go about it? What steps can we take? It requires action, determination, and consistency. It might require a substantial attitude change. The key to becoming motivated is to understand the importance of the opportunity to make a difference!

GO THE EXTRA MILE

Go the extra mile in preparing for rehearsals. Of course you can "get by" with little preparation, but don't expect anything special to come out of that rehearsal. Go the extra mile by allowing your imagination free reign to come up with ideas: for how to teach the music, for how to motivate your choir, for how to work more effectively with difficult choir members, for how to pace rehearsals better, for more effective seating arrangements, and so on. Keep a small notebook with you at all times to capture those ideas when they first drift into your mind. Many good ideas are forgotten because they didn't get written down.

CARRY THROUGH ON PROMISES

Always do what you say you will. Holding out carrots in front of your choir—such as a weekend out-of-town choir trip or singing a special concert with instruments—will motivate only if the singers trust you to do what you say.

BE OPEN-MINDED

Be open-minded about changing rules and policies if a situation develops that makes the change beneficial. Consider what is in the best interests of all those concerned. Look at situations from other people's perspectives before you make decisions.

WHEN YOU MAKE A MISTAKE

If you make a mistake or are in the wrong about something you said or how you treated someone, admit it right away. If the choir encounters a problem because of what you know was your own mistake, make sure the choir knows that it wasn't their fault. This keeps them from feeling that they let you down, and it creates a sense of integrity and respect in your relationship. Self-deprecation is rare and respected.

Incidentally, everybody has bad days and everybody makes mistakes. Learn something from it, analyze probable causes, and move on. Once you have gleaned what you can from the past, close your mind to it and quit fretting about what cannot be changed. Have the grace to adjust and get on with a more positive outlook.

WHEN WE TALLY UP HOW WE DID

There will inevitably come a time when we will look back at our choir directing days and tally up how we did. When that day comes, what do we want that record to show? Will we have made the most of every opportunity to make a difference? Will we have helped create all the beauty that was possible? Were singers and audiences or congregations uplifted by our efforts? Were we all that we could have been? Is the world a better place because we passed through? Think ahead to how you would like to answer those questions and begin now to make your time count each day and every rehearsal.

CHAPTER 19

STEPS TOWARD INCREASING YOUR EFFECTIVENESS

BECOME A POWERFUL MOTIVATOR

Would you like to be a better "people person," a more powerful motivator to your singers? Get an image in your mind of what such a person would be like. Perhaps you are already thinking of someone you know who has those very characteristics. If you want to be like that person, mentally become that person. Visualize the image of those personality characteristics you so admire and desire for yourself, and step into that picture—begin acting that part. Create the vision and simply start becoming it . . . with the help of a little imagination.

SIMPLIFY YOUR LIFE

Simplifying your life can be an important personal motivator. Having more on your plate than one can possibly do well inhibits motivation. To become a highly motivated and more fulfilled person, you may have to do fewer things, allowing you to concentrate on your priorities! No matter how hard we work or how talented we are, it takes time to be creative and thorough. So consider doing less quantity for the sake of more quality. Take a careful look at your schedule. Are you investing significant time in activities or interests that do not take you closer to your hopes and dreams for your life? Have you slipped into the rut of doing so much for others that you haven't had time for your own secret hopes for accomplishment? Search out at least some peripheral activities that don't contribute to the big goals in your life. Put your own priorities first. In the big picture, that approach will eventually serve others better. Some of the activities you may have to eliminate may be ones you enjoy, but if they do not take you closer to your life goals, there are more significant ways to spend your time. When you realize the majority of your day is being spent in peripheral activities, it's time to simplify and to focus on what is really important.

GUARD AGAINST EXHAUSTION

Burning the candle at both ends lately? You can't begin to climb out of a rut without first getting a decent night's sleep. An exhausted mind and body are not conducive to resiliency. Once you get some needed rest, think through your typical schedule and search out the pressure spots that put you in such an exhausted state. Take some steps to ease those pressure areas. Can you delegate some responsibilities that do not require your unique expertise or education? Do all those tasks really need to be done? What would the result be if you did fewer things, but did them better?

EVALUATE YOUR STRENGTHS AND WEAKNESSES

Do an inventory of your strengths and weaknesses. Our tendency is to keep working on our areas of strength but to ignore our weak areas. Are you extremely creative but woefully disorganized? Are you adept at the piano but awkward and inexperienced as a singer? Do you tend to be efficient in rehearsals but not naturally inspirational—or vice versa? When there are minisessions at a conference, most conductors attend the sessions in which they are already strong, instead of dealing realistically with their weaknesses. Consider choosing a few specific areas in which you do not feel confident to work on over the next six months and list some steps you can take. Keep a journal of your growth in these areas. Make a note on your calendar twice a month to check your own progress. The path to excellence is built not only on your strengths, but also on your determination to become more complete.

What are your personal strengths as a conductor? Play to those strengths. For example, if you have a strong vocal background, work through your choir with mini–voice lessons. If you have a strong interest in history, work into your rehearsals concise but interesting background on the texts and/or composers for each rehearsal. If you have a strong keyboard background, record the accompaniments of major works and make them available to choir members for home preparation. But use your strengths to make being in your choir uniquely effective in those areas.

VIDEOTAPE A REHEARSAL

Set goals for yourself as a conductor. Videotape a rehearsal and choose one or two things you would like to do better. Perhaps it is your demeanor, the color and pacing of your speaking voice, the way you stand, the size of your conducting gestures, the percentage of rehearsal time you tend to talk as opposed to letting the choir sing. Don't try to fix everything at once! Just one or two ideas that can be a personal, private goal in the back of your mind while you conduct. But keep a record of your progress. You will find both these ideas to be highly motivating, and you will find yourself looking forward to that next rehearsal.

DEVELOP MINIGOALS

Develop personal minigoals for your own conducting technique and vocal production, and find ways of keeping them constantly in mind. Write them out on little cards and get into the habit of pulling them out several times a day, e.g., when you are on hold on the phone, when you are waiting for someone to show up, or when a discussion doesn't pertain to you. Tape them on your home and office mirrors and on your music stand. Perhaps choose one choral and one personal goal to concentrate on next rehearsal. Keep a journal of daily progress on these goals.

KEEP A CONDUCTOR'S JOURNAL

Keep a daily conductor's journal similar to that suggested in *The Artist's Way: A Spiritual Path to Higher Creativity* by Julia Cameron (New York: Penguin Putnam, Inc., 2002). Remind yourself of ways in which you have made a positive difference in people's lives and in the community. What are you proud of? What incremental steps might you still take to learn, to grow, to be more sensitive, and to reach out to others? It is the small, steady steps forward that lead to wisdom, effectiveness, and personal peace.

KEEP A RECORD OF GROWTH

Keep a record of growth in the choral program and improvement in the sound of the choir. Such growth is often so gradual that both administrators and choir fail to realize the significance of what happened. Keep a record of what the program was like before you began to rebuild it, e.g., how many were in the choirs, audio tapes of their sound before you started working this season, perhaps a unison singing of "My Country, 'Tis of Thee" or a well-known hymn. Also indicate what impact the choir had on the larger institution. Then halfway through the season, do a comparative overview. Record a few lines from the same music, compare numbers of participants, include quotes from choir members about how the year is going, and note ways that the choir program has supported other segments of the institution (see chapter 27). Let the choirs hear their own change in sound; they will already be excited about the growth in numbers. Consider sharing the comparisons with your administrators as a part of periodic evaluations.

CONTINUE TO LEARN

Leaders have a voracious appetite for learning. They want to learn all they can about every aspect of their professions. Choral conductors should study books on choral conducting to see what helpful ideas may be there; they should call or e-mail experienced conductors or former college professors for other ideas. As they learn, they try out new ideas and evaluate the results. They try to keep their insights fresh, and those who work under them or sing under them are intrigued and stimulated by the resulting vitality—so different from the same old thing each rehearsal.

DEVELOP A BRAIN TRUST SUPPORT SYSTEM

Nurture relationships with a few trusted friends or colleagues who could serve as your support system in your personal growth journey. If no one knows about your secret hopes, dreams, and goals, it is all too easy to let the dreams slip away amidst the press of life. So share those private aspirations with these caring friends and associates, asking them to help you keep moving towards your goals. Having the encouragement and support of others helps keep you on track.

Develop a similar brain trust with other teachers and conductors carefully chosen for their positive and uplifting styles. Get together several times a year when it helps the most—perhaps early summer when you can share repertoire and special activity ideas for the coming season, and in mid-November and late January when most of us are worn thin and in need of a pick-me-up. You might have to go a distance to find the kind of inspirational directors with whom this would be an effective and helpful experience, but it is well worth it. Don't know whom to ask? Contact your own college or organizations like the American Choral Directors Association or the Choristers Guild for the names of vibrant, successful directors in your general vicinity, and then give them a call.

CHAPTER 20

STUCK IN A RUT?

ARE YOU SURE SOMETHING IS WRONG?

A rut is not a crisis. It is more a lack of freshness and spontaneity in your day-to-day regimen. Nothing in particular is wrong. It's just that you catch yourself looking at the clock during rehearsals. You are less engaged, easily distracted, with a tendency to get off track and talk too much. You find yourself too often just getting by instead of working toward real beauty. Your creative juices aren't flowing, and no "ah-hahs" are on the horizon. Routine has settled in, and each rehearsal seems about the same. Your choir members can all guess how you will rehearse each piece, and there is nothing to keep them on the edges of their seats. That's being in a rut. The good news is that ruts are usually the result of things going pretty well. Since there are no fires to put out, you get lulled into a "business as usual" mind set, and that demotivates both conductors and singers.

AVOID BLAMING YOURSELF

Avoid blaming yourself when you find yourself in a rut. It isn't necessarily because of anything you did or failed to do. It may be due to circumstances beyond your control. You may have been distracted by personal matters or institutional politics. You might have gone through a particularly busy period when you were overwhelmed with work and were consistently short on sleep. You may not be getting the encouragement or support of your bosses. We all go through some of those times, but eventually, for the sake of all those who depend upon you for inspiration and beauty in their lives, you have to climb out. Don't waste time fretting about how you got into a rut. Just take some positive steps to get out!

LOSE THE BLAHS

Lose your blahs by losing yourself in others, by making rehearsals wonderful for your singers. The blahs often stem from thinking too selfishly about yourself. When you pour yourself out for the sake of others, it's hard to keep that smile off your face.

TAKE TIME OUT

Take some time out to recharge your creative juices. If we fill every moment with busyness, there is no time for reflection, for dreaming up new ways to approach the music, to make rehearsals interesting. It takes time to be creative. Don't fill up every moment with more stuff. Resist the temptation to have the television on or music playing continually. Allow silence to free your imagination to wander. Schedule some daily time when your brain does not have to work on something specific and let it simply mull things over. Stop "accomplishing" long enough to dream up fresh possibilities that might intrigue you and give your work new zest. You will be surprised how quickly new ideas come your way.

LEARN TO STEP AWAY

The typical choir director—a mile-a-minute dynamo—flips from one rehearsal or meeting to the next, pressing, pressing, pressing. Learn to step away every once in a while for moments of quiet meditation. Schedule in fifteen minutes alone before rehearsals with no interruptions. After several hours of high-intensity work, step outside and take a short walk. I know a successful swim coach who religiously takes a long walk in the middle of each day. He says walking soothes his soul, makes him a better coach, breaks the tension, helps him keep things in perspective, and lets him come up with solutions to concerns. Creativity and inspiration come in those quiet moments of peace. Make stepping away a part of your daily routine.

CHOOSE YOUR FRIENDS CAREFULLY

Think about the people with whom you spend a lot of time. Write down their names and candidly assess the effect they have on your mood. Are they positive, upbeat, vital, optimistic, creative "can do" people who are supportive and encouraging to you in your life? Or are they pessimistic and cynical, defeatist "why bother" people who tend to pull you down to their moods? The attitudes of your friends are contagious. They can lift up your spirits or pull you down. If you want to be a highly motivated person, make a conscious decision to spend more time with positive people and less time with negative people.

CARRY AROUND PEARLS OF WISDOM

For those moments that all of us have when we need a little extra inspiration, carry small cards in your wallet with inspirational pearls of wisdom, reminders of our foundational beliefs. It's an effective way to overcome doubts, fears, and nervousness. One of my favorite cards borrows from Henry David Thoreau:

- Take time by the forelock, now or never (i.e., strike while the iron is hot).
- Only fools stand on their island of opportunities and look toward another land.
- Launch yourself on every wave.
- People were born to succeed, not to fail.

WALL OF HEROES

What wall in your office or rehearsal room is the one you notice the most? Use it for a "Wall of Heroes." Find photos of people you admire—professional conductors, mentors, college professors who meant a lot to you, workshop clinicians who made a strong impact on you—and hang those photos on your heroes' wall. When you need a little extra inspiration, spend some time soaking up what it is about each one that makes him or her so special. Then try to make those qualities a part of the person you want to be. When you go into the next rehearsal or meeting, you won't be alone.

CHAPTER 21

GETTING READY FOR REHEARSALS

How much importance do you attach to each rehearsal? As much as a performance? What would happen if you worked at making each rehearsal your masterpiece? Why put off that surge of inspiration and self-motivation that comes almost magically just before a performance? Make "now" something to celebrate! Pretend that "This is it!" every rehearsal. The only difference between a rehearsal and a performance should be that in the latter you let audiences listen. For the choir, though, every rehearsal should be a thrill a minute!

MOTIVATION THROUGH BETTER REPERTOIRE PLANNING

The most significant choral motivator is the music you choose for your choir. Quality music of a reasonable level of difficulty and in a variety of moods and styles gives depth to your program. Music of substance is more interesting to rehearse and retains a better level of concentration than fluff. It also sticks with your choir members for life.

So be aware of difficulty levels and enticement value when planning music for the year. Avoid ulcers for yourself and your choir members resulting from music that is too hard with too little time to learn it, or too many difficult pieces scheduled in a row or on the same program. Consider both the difficulty of every piece of music and the enjoyment the choir will have singing it, and strive for balance. Take time to evaluate how many rehearsals it will take to prepare. Then give each piece of music a grade in both categories. Use a scale of 4 to 1, 4 being the highest grade and 1 being the lowest. As you consider repertoire, make sure that your choir members will immediately have a positive reaction to a majority of the music, and that each more difficult number is surrounded by several easier ones. This also keeps choir directors out of the black hole of extending rehearsals and scheduling extra ones because the choir couldn't get the music learned. When choir members work hard, the most common reason that the scheduled music is not ready is unrealistic planning by the conductor.

SPECIAL EVENTS THAT MOTIVATE

Develop a Christmas Eve, graduation, or other special event tradition of having one of the members of the choir conduct a piece. In preparation for choosing that person, spend some of your rehearsal time teaching the entire choir the conducting basics. Spend ample time with the chosen student conductor so that he or she is thoroughly prepared before working with the choir for the first time. The result is that the program or service becomes energized, and the singers become completely focused on watching and supporting whoever is conducting.

SETTING UP THE REHEARSAL ROOM

Make the rehearsal room look inviting and enticing. Arrange the chairs, risers, piano, tables for handing out music, and the like as carefully as you would prepare your home for a party. Get rid of all clutter. Give the walls a new paint job, using colors that that are calm but not dull. Check the temperature and the airflow in the rehearsal room. If the lighting is old and insufficient, do all you can to have new fixtures installed. These enhancements say to your choir members that they are important and that you are doing all you can to make choir special for them.

CHOIR DYNASTY BULLETIN BOARD

Develop a "Choir Dynasty" bulletin board that honors your choir's history and traditions. Include quotes from both current and former choir members about what singing in the choir has meant to them, including the individual's name below each quote. Include collages of photos from previous choir retreats, tours, and other special choir events. If the choir doesn't have a history yet, start one.

EXACT SEATING CHARTS

Have an exact seating chart posted for every rehearsal and train singers of all age choirs to check the chart when they enter. Occasionally switch around seating positions according to the needs of the main piece for that rehearsal. Seeing one's name on the chart helps singers feel they really belong and their contributions are valued.

BUILDING BLOCKS FOR CHORAL SUCCESS

Put the "Building Blocks of Choral Success" (see figure 21.1) on the wall or on a pull-down screen for mid-rehearsal reference and motivational reminder. Feel free to vary my category suggestions to your own needs. Explain how our vocal, dramatic, and enunciation skills rely completely on the basics found on the lower level: alertness, reliability, cooperation, and initiative. When the need arises in rehearsal, point to the problem area and say, "Are you doing your part to make this the best choir it can be? We can't do it without your great contribution. Be all you can be! Help us be all we can be!"

BUILDING BLOCKS FOR CHORAL SUCCESS

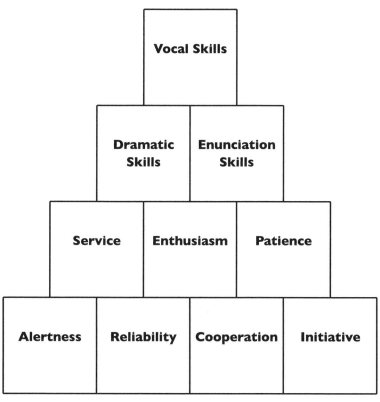

Copyright 2004 Michael E. Kemp

Figure 21.1

TAKE A CHOIR PHOTOGRAPH

Take a choir photo early in the year to be displayed with individuals identified by name below the photo. This can help shy choir members learn the names of others.

MOTIVATE THROUGH DAILY INFORMATION SHEETS

Before rehearsal place on the choir chairs half-page information sheets containing interesting information about the first piece to be rehearsed that day (e.g., facts about the composer, a related historical perspective, anticipated problems of which the singers should be aware, text explanations or translations, translations of musical terms). When choir members arrive, they will use their time constructively by learning about the first anthem to be rehearsed, which will heighten their interest and motivate them to give more of themselves.

CHAPTER 22

A SUCCESSFUL REHEARSAL COMES FROM A STIMULATING PLAN

THE FIRST REHEARSAL OF THE SEASON

Group e-mails. On an information card for all members to fill out in the first rehearsal of the season, include a request for e-mail addresses (see figure 22.1). Urge those who don't have e-mail to consider it (several free e-mail options exist), because you plan to send out a group e-mail to the choir the day after most rehearsals. In this e-mail you can included comments about what went well last rehearsal and what needs improvement, perhaps some interesting tidbit about one of the pieces on which you have been working, schedule reminders, what piece is the most important for next rehearsal, and encouragement to work a little on their own. Depending upon the nature and purpose of your choir, this last statement could be an assignment, rather than a casual suggestion. If you have children's or youth choirs, also request e-mail addresses for their parents. Keeping the parents in the loop will prove invaluable.

COMMUNITY CHOIR   2008–2009 SEASON

Name: _____

Adult: _____ or Student: _____ (grade: _____)

E-mail address: _____

Parents' e-mail address if student: _____

Voice part: _____

Height: _____

Please inform the director of any changes during the season.

Thank you.

Figure 22.1

Candid photos. Have candid photos taken during the first rehearsals and at least once a month for your "Choir Dynasty" bulletin board (see chapter 21). Try to have the photographer not be one of the singers; you need your leaders singing. When the photos are displayed, label the names of the people in each photo to help choir members get to know one another.

Record their first sounds. Try this approach within a rehearsal early in the season. Record the choir singing a familiar anthem, hymn, or "My Country, 'Tis of Thee" before you do any warming up, polishing, or skill building. Then after fixing their posture, building their sound, deepening their tone color, working on phrasing, enunciation, style of articulation, and adding dramatic flair, record them again. Play both versions and challenge your choir to make that much difference on every piece of music they sing.

PLANNING DAILY OR WEEKLY CHORAL GOALS

Choose one problem of the day or week to emphasize throughout a rehearsal, a bit like *Sesame Street* chooses one letter or one number of the day. The subject could be any choral or musical skill: e.g., careful tuning, clearer consonants, blending your voice with others, dynamic control, better vocal habits, or developing a more sustained line. Emphasize that discipline throughout that rehearsal. Write it on the board in big letters. At the end of the rehearsal, ask choir members to describe what they have learned about the "problem of the day." Have them sing a phrase or two correctly; then the same phrase wrong; then the same phrase correctly again. Tell them that the responsibility for that skill is now theirs. Try building up some anticipation by announcing near the end of the rehearsal, "Come ready next week for our next 'Skill of the Day,' _____."

TWO SUGGESTED METHODS FOR SETTING THE REHEARSAL ORDER

The importance of having some plan for each rehearsal can't be stressed enough. Try one of these.

The "Sonata Allegro" Planning Form. Plan your rehearsal agenda according to the sonata-allegro form, as suggested by Lawrence Kaptein in a *Choral Journal* article (November 1987).

According to this creative approach, in the *exposition* of the rehearsal, the first third, you should establish direction, enthusiasm, and momentum. This segment should include short pedagogical (teaching) drills chosen for their relationship to the needs of the first piece to be rehearsed. Following this, work at a fairly quick pace through several selections on which you do not anticipate major concerns. It is important not to get bogged down in this first third of the rehearsal. Letting your choir sing through several pieces without interrupting in this first part of the rehearsal gives your choir a sense of accomplishment. Success in these easier initial tasks increases their confidence and their enthusiasm, and paves the way for increased capacity for the complex learning ahead.

The middle part of the rehearsal, the so-called *development* section, is a time of growing intensity and expectation. The rehearsal becomes intentionally slower and more focused. Because of the successes of the exposition, the singers are now ready for the challenge of a more detailed and diligent rehearsal. Work on only one or two selections in this more intense manner—perhaps only a portion of each.

The last major portion of the rehearsal, the *recapitulation*, is a period of summation, evaluation, reflection, and reinforcement. It is a time to give the choir a sense of worth about good things that happened in the rehearsal as well as an opportunity to talk about what the group can hope to do better next rehearsal.

Consider a short final period in your rehearsals, a *codetta*: Pass out "dessert"—one of the choir's favorite pieces from the past—let them sing it without further comment from you, and then send them out smiling . . . perhaps even a minute before the scheduled ending.

The Graph of Natural Focus in Parts of Rehearsals. Plan according to the natural Graph of the Ability to Concentrate in Rehearsals (see figure 22.2). There is a norm to the innate ability to concentrate that choir members bring to various segments of a typical rehearsal, be it forty-five minutes or two hours. When choir members arrive, they are usually scattered and unfocused, so the most effective beginning to most rehearsals is some type of warm-up that builds discipline and synergism (ensemble), moving them toward singing well. Follow this warm-up with an opening piece of music that calls for rich, vibrant singing. The most effective concentration capacity in a typical rehearsal is at about the one-fourth mark, the time when the most significant and complex work can be accomplished. So follow the opening vibrant piece with music that requires brainy, focused thinking. The halfway mark in rehearsals slides down somewhat in productivity, and the low point in concentration falls just after the halfway mark, five-eighths of the way through rehearsal. Of all the pieces scheduled for this rehearsal, choose for this spot the one which choir members love the most. Singing something they love will rekindle needed energy for the last fourth of the rehearsal. The last ten minutes of the rehearsal become increasingly less productive, because singers' minds begin to shift to whatever is next on their own schedules. Use this time to review what you have learned this rehearsal, perhaps sing a few of those places one last time, go over what went well and what will be the focus of the next rehearsal. After a few closing words of appreciation for their good efforts, you can close by passing out "dessert" as mentioned in the sonata-allegro plan described above.

GRAPH OF NATURAL FOCUS IN PARTS OF REHEARSALS

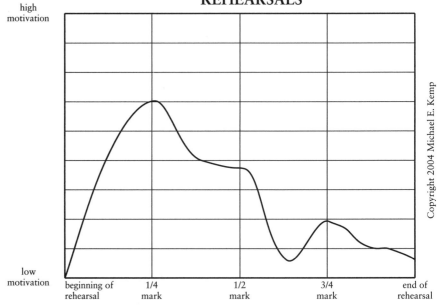

Figure 22.2

THE END OF THE SEASON

Toward the end of a season, we tend to sweep problems under the carpet of "I'll think about it later," but we seldom remember the specifics when it is time to plan the next season. Take time at the end of each season to make a serious evaluation of everything having to do with your program:

- What went well?
- What problems or disappointments were there?
- How did the repertoire choices work out?
- How was administrative efficiency (e.g., planning of tours, music processing, attendance, grading, communication with accompanist, adult helpers, students, administrative supervisors)?
- How was the balance between building skills and learning music on the one hand, and building relationships and motivating on the other?

CHAPTER 23

KEEPING REHEARSALS ALIVE

PRIOR TO THE REHEARSAL

Sensitize your ears. Many athletes watch videos of champions for inspiration just prior to their own matches. The videos set the image of greatness in their minds, helping them raise the expectations they have of themselves. Indeed, they feel those champions within themselves and use that as inspiration to play "above their heads." Diamond cutters carry a perfect gem in their pockets, and they stop every once in a while to study that perfection, to urge themselves toward similar great expectations. For fifteen minutes before rehearsals, play CDs of great performances to set your own aural standards as high as possible. Don't play it as background music while you do other busy work, but actually *listen*. Notice details of tuning, blending, and rhythmic ensemble; then listen just as carefully to your own choirs in rehearsal. Trust your ears and follow your instincts to move your choirs toward higher refinement.

Be a great host. Arrive at rehearsal early enough to get the necessary organizational details out of the way before any choir members arrive. This allows you to welcome your choir members as a good host, making a positive and caring start to the rehearsal—for example, "It's good to see you here. You make a difference. Thanks in advance for the great job you are going to do today in rehearsal." When the first choir members arrive, be available, approachable, compelling—and do the same after rehearsal. Make it clear that you want to get to know them better.

BEGINNING THE REHEARSAL

Bright starts. The beginning of rehearsals should be so stimulating, enticing, and enjoyable that it makes arriving promptly well worth the effort. You want those who tend to come late to eventually realize that they are missing out on something special. Often, the opening minutes of rehearsals are more or less wasted because of disorganization, waiting for more members to show up, or a poorly planned, underenergized first idea. The briskness, efficiency, and warmth of the opening greeting must be carefully thought out and carried off. This should be followed by some physically stimulating stretches and an easy-to-teach warm-up matched functionally to the first piece to be rehearsed.

Planning warm-ups. Warm-ups basically exist for only two purposes: vocal preparation for better singing and specific problem solving. Regarding the first, exercises should be simple and emphasize posture, getting the breath moving, and vocal placement (the quality of the sound). Regarding the second, problem solving, each piece of music has unique inherent problems, and therefore the warm-ups should vary according to the needs of the first piece to be rehearsed. All warm-ups should be easy to learn, and the entire process should not take up too much rehearsal time, certainly no more than five minutes.

Get them singing. Start on time and get the choir singing right away. Talking too much at first creates a sluggish start to any rehearsal. This style of quick start is one of the secrets to the game show *Jeopardy.* Consider always beginning with the same short piece of music, beautiful to sing and to listen to, which can be memorized early in the season. Choir members can then participate in the opening music of the rehearsal, even if they are not quite in their places yet. This also becomes a sign that the work of the rehearsal is beginning, a far better opening shot than the director shouting, [Clap! Clap!] "Come on now; you should already be in your seats. We've got to get started!"

Bold beginnings. Urge your singers not to be tentative at the beginning of rehearsal. Your singers' first warm-up notes (or whatever singing sounds they first make at a rehearsal) should be like a firm handshake or a high five. Such confidence awakens the body under the voice, and the resulting compression is the beginning of breath support, which is so important to warming up the voice. As in sports, overcoming this initial tentativeness opens the doors of enjoyment and effectiveness, and that joy of singing becomes a lasting motivator.

DURING THE REHEARSAL

Make rehearsals special. When you throw a party at your house, what do you do? You clean it and make it look inviting. You make a special effort to look your best. Is your choir important enough to warrant going out of your way to make things special for them? Are they important enough for you to look your best and present a vibrant, uplifting countenance? These extra efforts make your choir members—your guests—feel welcome and honored, and that makes them want to give their all back to you. Play the consummate host.

Eliciting greater effort. Ask a lot of your choir. Great results come from great effort, and not just from you. There are no miracles, only hard work with well-earned payoffs. Work your choir hard, but then make sure they hear and sense the difference. On a quality scale of 1 to 10 (10 being the best), have them sing a section of music at a 4, just below average. Then challenge them—one time—to sing the same section as close to 10 as they can get. They will like the sound. They will rise to the occasion. For high school or college choirs, try using a scale of age levels, rather than numbers—e.g., sing this section, say, as a choir of 14-year-olds; now as a choir of 18-year-olds; now as a choir of college seniors. Have a discussion about how the different levels felt to them. Chances are, they liked being that good.

Share purpose. Briefly mention why you do certain things in rehearsals. For instance, you may warm up a certain way to develop the particular style of the first anthem to be rehearsed. You may rehearse refrains first, since they appear several times during the anthem, and then you do not have to work on them each time they appear. You may work to develop a different tone color for Palestrina than Brahms, and it is more interesting to choir members if they know why. If they understand the uniqueness of that purpose, they will work harder at doing it well. But make these explanations short and clear; extended intellectual lectures erode rehearsal efficiency and may bore singers.

Hold attention with variety. Keep your rehearsals interesting by changing the music or section on which you are working every once in a while. The secret of *Sesame Street* is that they use lots of short segments, and viewers never get bored. To work on one section of one piece for an entire rehearsal can burn singers out.

One thing at a time. When you hear much that needs to be fixed, use what the business world calls the salami approach. Cut what you hear into palatable slices. You can't fix it all, but what steps could you take to start the process of refinement? Either choose one skill per piece of music, changing for each piece of music, or choose two skills to use throughout rehearsal on all the music as a way to incorporate better habits. Don't hit your singers with everything you know, especially after attending an inspiring workshop that leaves you eager to try out new ideas.

Grab that attention back. Here's a handy game that requires quick reactions and total concentration. Explain the game and allow the choir to hear a selected target pitch. Rather than use an A, I suggest the more useful and vocally comfortable F. Then at the first sign of inattentiveness during rehearsal, hold up your hand with five fingers spread, then go to four, three, two, one, and finally a balled fist. At the balled-fist sign, choir members should sing the target pitch, to see how close they can come to it on the spur of the moment. Then get right back to work. You can use this successfully three or four times a rehearsal to capture and restore attention, and lose only fifteen seconds each time. You are also building what I refer to as "ballpark perfect pitch," which pays dividends when reading any music.

Memorable successes. In rehearsals, make a big thing of successes. When things go well, make sure the choir knows, but make a small thing of skills that still need work or areas in the music that still need attention. It is easy to slip into saying nothing when you are pleased, assuming the singers know it, and going overboard with what isn't working yet. Choir members thrive on affirmation, and get defeatist about overemphasized concerns.

Never give up. What about handling those rehearsals when nothing is working well, and you begin to feel overwhelmed with pessimism? No matter what that state is, your only concern should be what step you can take in the right direction. However poorly things are going, the process is not about achieving perfection so much as moving steadily toward it. Even if the sound or attitude is terrible, don't give up. Never, never give up the fight! Take some action to move things in a good direction. Then you can and should feel good after rehearsal. More than that, if each rehearsal takes steps in the right direction, your choir will eventually be the choir you want it to be.

Teaching sight-singing. For the longer-term problem of teaching your choir members to read music better, consider a Saturday sight-singing workshop once or twice a year at which you teach less-experienced singers the basics: the names of the pitches, how to determine keys, how to tell what the tonic is, how relating the notes to the tonic can help you find the pitch, the arithmetic of rhythm, and so on. During rehearsals, make it part of your routine to ask your choir about the key and tonic, explain any Italian or other musical terms in the score, and urge them to ask about anything they see that they don't understand. This hooks them intellectually and keeps them much more attentive.

ENDING THE REHEARSAL

Seventh-inning stretch. Depending on the length of your rehearsals, make a tradition of giving your singers a "seventh-inning stretch" ten to fifteen minutes before the rehearsal is over. The idea is that once that stretch is over (actually have choir members stand and stretch), we make that final bit of rehearsal the best we possibly can, and thus leave with a sense of accomplishment. It would be a good idea to make any necessary announcements or reminders about the importance of their commitment, attendance, promptness, and overall reliability during the seventh-inning stretch; then end rehearsal singing rather than talking.

What did they learn? Toward the end of a particularly effective rehearsal, have your choir members write out insights gained in their own singing and musicality, e.g., vocal techniques or certain phrasing ideas that made a significant difference to them. Have them place that list in their folders where they will see it every rehearsal. Take a moment in each rehearsal for the singers to reread those ideas, adding new thoughts each week. They become intrigued with writing their own teaching guide, and retention of concepts becomes the norm.

Assignments. Even in volunteer choirs, make assignments for those who are able to work on music on their own. At the close of each rehearsal, tell your choir what is the most important music on tap for the next rehearsal. Say how much it would mean to the speed, efficiency, and quality of the rehearsal if those who are able would look at this music in advance. This also reminds singers that you are working hard for them.

AFTER THE REHEARSAL

How did you do? Immediately after each rehearsal, write down for yourself your candid evaluations of that rehearsal in a journal, indicating which anthems and procedures went well and which didn't. Continue the approaches that worked well, change those that crashed, and modify those that almost worked well. Consider evaluating right on the sheet you use for planning rehearsals. Did the timing work out as anticipated? Did you get to all the music you hoped to? Were you adequately prepared? Were there any surprises that you could anticipate next time? How effective were your warm-ups, and how much time did they take from note learning? Use this information to plan your next rehearsal. It is usually best to plan that next rehearsal agenda soon after this rehearsal, when these thoughts are fresh. Keep an ongoing current rehearsal agenda on your computer's desktop, simply revising it week to week.

Sending group e-mails. Let's reexamine for a moment the idea of e-mails to the choir, first mentioned in chapter 22. After every rehearsal (or, in the case of multiple rehearsals a week, on a weekly basis), send a group e-mail to your choir, so that they know that each rehearsal is important and that its successes and difficulties are significant. Tell them of your gratitude for their commitment to the choir and for all their hard work. Applaud a few things that really went well in rehearsal, and then suggest one or two things on which to concentrate next time. According to the above-mentioned rehearsal evaluation, list what will be most helpful regarding their note preparation for next rehearsal. End with "Looking forward to seeing you there!" It is imperative that these postrehearsal choir e-mails not be too long. People tend to read short paragraphs but trash long epistles.

Absentee follow-ups. Send an immediate personal e-mail to anyone who has an unexpected absence, saying how important they are to the choir and how much they are missed when they aren't there. If it is a sensitive relationship, call instead. Express concern that they are okay, assuming that when they aren't at choir they might be ill or have some other serious concern. If that is the case, ask if there is anything you or the choir could do to help. If everything is okay—they just didn't make it for whatever reason—wish them well and tell them you look forward to seeing them next week. When the word spreads that you will be contacting each unscheduled absentee, choir members won't miss casually.

I'm always surprised when I contact a missing choir member to hear the reply, "I didn't know I made a difference." Emphasize teamwork with your choirs. Each member must feel ownership, pride, a sense of personal responsibility, and a sense that each one makes a difference. Avoid the sentiment that the "stars" are the only important members of the choir. Every person makes a significant contribution.

Charming notes. Send out at least three "charming notes" (see chapter 32) to individual choir members after every rehearsal. Keep a record of those to whom you write so that you eventually get through the entire choir. This personal touch of a short handwritten note deepens your individual relationships with singers and their dedication to the choir. If it is simpler for you, use e-mail. The added advantage of e-mail is that you often get a lovely response back, since it is so easy for the recipient to do; that back-and-forth begins to build strong relationships and a higher level of commitment from singers.

Follow up on concerns. If during rehearsal you notice someone who seems tense, upset, or simply uninspired, give him or her a call at home after rehearsal. "You seemed a little down today. Is everything okay?" Usually your phone call is much appreciated. The tension probably had nothing to do with you, but the fact that you cared enough to call could mean the world to that choir member.

CHAPTER 24

TEACHING THROUGH SPORTS ANALOGIES

We live in a society that is inundated with sports. Since sports images are so pervasive today, sports analogies are an effective way to explain certain elements of vocal and musical concepts.

In the following analogies, the singers' part is in parentheses.

GENERAL SPORTS ANALOGIES

- A fiberglass pole flings pole-vaulters over the bar (the sustaining, forward-thrusting feeling of well-placed and supported singing).
- Joggers look far ahead and not at their feet (singers should look farther down the phrase when reading and for more sensitive phrasing).
- Ping-pong strokes have a crisp initial hit with a smooth follow through (singers need to initiate a note with the clarity of staccato but with the smooth follow-through of legato).

SPECIFIC TENNIS ANALOGIES

- Arrive early enough to stretch, warm up, and focus your thoughts (arrive early enough to get physically prepared and mentally focused; avoid too much casual chit-chat just before rehearsal begins—for singers and conductors).
- A tennis player's alertness and stance when receiving a serve (singers' physical connection and alertness).
- Firm, but not stiff, grip on racket (firm, but not stiff, support).
- Get your body ready with "split steps"—a little jump just as your opponent hits the ball—to break the inertia and get you moving (get ready vocally and physically to sing; take time to relax the abdomen and then resupport every time you take a breath).
- Aim for the back line to keep opponents on the defensive (target emphases further down the phrase).

- Don't slap at the ball; hit *through* it (avoid staccato attacks that stop the momentum; instead, sing through the note or phrase smoothly).
- Brush up and forward on the ball (sing with high, forward placement).
- For an overhead smash, hit up and through the ball (when you go for a high note, avoid banging into its initiation; rather, drive through it to the following note).
- Finish the stroke completely by ending with forward motion, not wrapping the racket around the body (keep the support and placement through the final consonant; avoid backing off prematurely).
- Keep your motions centered by using smaller, less flamboyant strokes (avoid the tendency to be too aggressive and dramatic, choosing rather to emphasize a more subtle artistry).
- Be aware of the whole court, where you, your partner, and your opponents are (be sensitive to the other voice parts and the accompaniment; listen while you sing).
- When you let down and play a point poorly, don't dwell on it; get on to the next point (when you realize you are straining or not singing sensitively, stop, take a breath, resupport, and go back to the basics).
- After a great point, game, or set, stay focused; avoid getting casual and cocky (when you are singing well, don't overdo it; don't sing too long or too hard).
- In sports, you can't afford to beat yourself up after a mistake; you can't let your frustration over something that happened on the previous point distract you from playing well on the next one (choral directors need to be resilient in the face of problems; look forward with vision and take positive steps toward that vision right now; learn from the past where possible, but don't get stuck there).
- Regardless of how things are going, let your enjoyment of the game be obvious; don't let competition make you negative (never let your singing—or conducting—slip into drudgery; let your enjoyment be obvious).

Take a page out of coaching vernacular: "It's not about having a great *voice*; it's all about character. Are you giving your personal all for the team? Striving for excellence is more important than the accident of natural talent."

These analogies are examples of correlations between singing and sports. To make this concept more useful and compelling for your choirs, think of analogies for the sports in which your choir members are involved or that you personally enjoy.

CHAPTER 25

PEOPLE SKILLS FOR CHOIR DIRECTORS

LEARN NAMES

Learn and remember names—and use those names often in rehearsals and in the hallways. In his world-renowned book *How to Win Friends and Influence People*, Dale Carnegie wrote that everyone's favorite word is his or her own name. When you call a person by name, he or she feels that you care about them; the atmosphere in the room is immediately warmer. With large choruses, learning names is a challenge. That's why the Choir Dynasty Bulletin Board is so useful. Have a photographer take photos for the first several rehearsals and have someone help identify the faces if you can't yet. With school choruses, you can photocopy individual photos of choir members from last year's yearbook. Photos of new students are usually available too. Cut out the photocopied pictures and put on three-by-five-inch cards with the names below the photo. Study these cards before every rehearsal until you know every choir member's name.

GIVE SINGERS YOUR FULL ATTENTION

Before and after rehearsals and during breaks, when your choir members say hello or want to chat, look at them and give them your full attention. We directors have so much going on that it is easy to be inadvertently superficial in these conversations. Undivided attention lets them know that they are important to you, and that will pay dividends. The secret is getting all the little administrative and planning things done in advance so that rehearsals can be about people.

THE CHORUS AS A SUPPORT SYSTEM

Keep choir members aware of each other's needs. Let people know when fellow choir members are going through hard times or facing a loss. Being in the choir should mean you are part of a family that cares. At the same time, also be sensitive to privacy issues.

GENUINE INTEREST IN YOUR CHOIR MEMBERS

Find out the special interests or hobbies of each of your choir members through a form that all members fill out at the beginning of each season. For those people whose interests relate to your own, make a point of linking up with them. Do some research on the interests less known to you, enough to initiate some conversation. When singers sense your interest in their passions, they feel validated, and the community ties with the choir are strengthened.

BE SENSITIVE TO FEELINGS

Always help choir members save face, and have your radar up for when you need to back off. Never single people out unless it is a quick, easy fix and you know that they can handle it. Get into the habit of watching your singers closely during rehearsals. Their faces, body language, and energy level are clear indicators about when you should move on to another piece, when the choir needs a short break, when you need to move faster or slower, and when individual singers need personal attention with vocal technique, note learning, or other such concerns. When personal attention is needed, ask the individual to give you a few minutes after rehearsal or set up a time to get together.

MAKE A BIG THING OF IMPROVEMENT

Praise even the slightest improvement, especially with a person or section that doesn't get many compliments (e.g., troublemakers and less surface-talented students). Everyone likes how a compliment feels, and they will do what they can to get more of the same. Point out and build on choir members' strengths, while encouraging growth in their weaker areas.

POSITIVE COMMENTS FIRST

Wrap comments in positives. Find something good to say about what the choir has just sung—"Great energy level," "That's terrific diction," or "You have a natural musicality in the way you sing that phrase"—before suggesting a correction or improvement. Remember to limit your corrections to no more than two so singers have a fighting chance to make the corrections successfully. Refer to those suggestions as something to add to what they already do well. Make them proud to be taking those steps forward.

IF ALL ELSE FAILS, MAKE IT UP!

Every once in a while there are moments in rehearsals when—let's face it—you can't find anything positive about the choir's singing on which to build. If you find yourself there, try this creative approach. Act as though a particular trait were there (even though it isn't; no one knows that but you). One example: "Only the tenors sang that phrase with the kind of energy that I need all of you to use. Sing that again for them, tenors." It works every time. The tenors rise admirably to the compliment (amazing as it seems); they now sing with tremendous energy, and everyone ends up singing better by their example!

CHAPTER 26

GETTING SINGERS TO AIM HIGHER

CHOIR MAKEOVERS

How about a choir makeover? Instead of using your continuing education money to go to a workshop somewhere else one year, use those funds to bring a clinician in for a weekend. Even better, take your choir (adult, college, or youth) to a retreat site for a workshop just for them on Friday evening through Saturday afternoon. Included could be full rehearsals of the highlights for the next half season, sectional rehearsals on notes, a short lecture about vocal technique, mini–voice lessons for every individual singer (some choirs like to do this in front of the whole choir, with everyone cheering everyone else on), brief and informal performances by smaller ensembles from within the choir, and a discussion about what it will take from the director and from the singers to make this a terrific year (see the next section).

DEVELOP GREAT EXPECTATIONS

Choir needs to be a two-way street of significant responsibility. We can only be a choir of which we are proud if we all keep the agreements and honor the responsibilities that we have set. When those commitments slip, by any of us for any reason, we should agree to face it together and discuss it openly and directly, one on one. That's how we care for one another; that's how we make choir something special.

In the first rehearsal of the season, ask your choir members these questions: Would you rather be a member of a terrific choir or a bad one? How would it make you feel to be in a choir that everyone bragged about? What will it take from you, the choir, to achieve those goals? What will it take from the director? Go through a process of listing specifically what it would take, putting each expectation on the board as you talk. Start with the expectations the choir members have of you. Let the choir members develop that list, giving them hints as necessary. Examples include: start and stop rehearsals on time, know the music, plan interesting rehearsals, be enthusiastic and friendly, listen to our suggestions. Then have the choir members develop expectations they should have of themselves: attend rehearsals regularly, arrive on time for rehearsals, keep a pencil in hand while singing, care about the details, sing with emotion. Have the results typed up and copied, and sign them during the next rehearsal. Choir members keep a signed copy of expectations they have of you, and you keep a signed copy of expectations they have agreed you should be able to have of them (and what they can expect from each other). Then if anyone does not fulfill his or her promise, pull out the agreement and have a private discussion. If the problem is broad-based, involve the entire choir. The expectations can be changed only by full choir discussion—and no one wants to tell the whole choir that they can't hold up their part of the bargain.

A More Profound Experience

Talk philosophically about not just singing, but using singing as a tool to create beauty. It's a little like going beyond just eating, and raising your sensitivities to really taste what you are eating. Urge your choir members to do more than go through the motions of singing, but to instead fill their singing with soul and understanding. Every time you sing, be a part of the beauty that is so desperately needed in today's world.

Share a Higher Purpose

For *church choirs*, talk about the important service you are providing and the importance of your contributions to worship. Talk theologically about giving generously of yourself to make a "worthy sacrifice." You might refer to the story at the end of the Second Book of Samuel about David's desire to make a worthy sacrifice, not one for which someone else does all the work. Remind the choir of the inspiration they are able to give to so many others.

In *school choirs*, talk about musical participation and understanding being a mark of sophistication and elegance, a sign of culture and refinement. Tie in the preparation of the music with related discussions about the texts and what they mean, or what life was probably like when these texts and the music were written (check out *The Timetables of History* by

Bernard Grun, published by Simon & Schuster, Inc., and similar resources), or the relationship between music and the visual arts of the period.

In *community choruses*, talk about what it means to be a community and how that is in essence what we model in a chorus. Talk about the need for beauty in today's world, and the opportunity we have of not only experiencing it for ourselves but also being able to bring that beauty to so many others in our community. Our music making lifts spirits and touches people deeply, including both ourselves and others.

KEEP THE FINAL PRODUCT IN MIND

Keep the choir thinking about the final product. How we use this rehearsal time now will make the difference in our eventual performance being gorgeous . . . or just so-so. Which do you want? There isn't any magic. Give it your best now and you will love the result. How good can you make it now? So let's rehearse as if this were the actual performance.

Watch the quality grow!

SPRINKLE IN MOTIVATIONAL STATEMENTS

To develop your singers' commitment and sense of responsibility to the choir, use phrases like "We are building a dynasty one person at a time"; "You are important to me and to this choir"; "Why do you take yourself less seriously than I do?"; "I never take your attendance or your contribution lightly."

YOU CAN DO IT!

When making corrections, make the fault seem easy to correct: "Come on, you can do this. . . . Try it again. . . . You're almost there." Directors can sometimes talk a problem to death, making it seem impossible to correct. So don't get bogged down with negatives. Inspire your singers with your confidence in them to achieve and conquer all problems.

CHAPTER 27

DEVELOPING TEAMWORK

LINKING UP WITH PHOTOS

For adults, develop a choir photo board with name, occupation, and hobby. For youth and children in church choirs, perhaps list their schools. For school choirs, list their grades. For college choirs, list their home states. Listing only names doesn't have the advantage of finding ways to link up with other choir members.

MYSTERY PERSON OF THE WEEK

To help choir members get to know each other better, institute a 2-minute "mystery choir member of the week" presentation mid-rehearsal (or preceding the break). The choir director has a phone conversation with an unannounced choir member during the week and finds out information about where the member grew up, their profession or special interests, singing or other musical background, or perhaps a short humorous story about them. During the presentation, the director describes that choir member without identifying the person's name until the end and finishes by saying, "Thank you, _____, for being in this choir and for all you give of yourself." The recipient feels honored and recommitted to the choir, and choir members get to know each other in a deeper way.

DEVELOPING CHOIR LEADERSHIP

Through the use of choir surveys and observation, note the talents of your individual choir members and other interested people in the congregation or institution, and create support-system jobs that match the talents you come up with. Library work, computer know-how, choir robe or concert attire maintenance, travel expertise, logistics coordinators, assistant accompanists, leadership for sectional rehearsals—all are areas in which volunteers could take pressure off you. Then let these future leaders see your sincerity, let them feel the worth of your belief in them, and let them feel they can make a difference.

HOW TO INCORPORATE NEW MEMBERS

In order to feel a part of the choir, new members need to be introduced, but doing so at the very beginning of rehearsal slows momentum. Try to get new members to come to their first rehearsal a little early. Introduce them to another person in their section who happens to be early, with instructions to take the newcomers under wing for the rehearsal. Just before the break, formally introduce the new members. Tell choir members that, before they chat with people they know during break, they should make the new members feel welcome.

Make joining the choir a memorable occasion for new members. Develop some type of welcome or induction ceremony after a new member comes for several weeks, which helps them understand the significance of becoming a member of the choir and the importance of their commitment. Stop rehearsal five minutes early. Have the choir stand in a circle with the new members in the middle. Each singer could be given a candle. The lights are lowered and the candles of choir members in the outer circle are lit. The conductor stresses that becoming a member of a choir is like joining a team or even a family. "We care about you . . . you can count on us . . . we are there for each other. Don't take us for granted, because we don't take you for granted." Then the choir should sing or hum a favorite melody like "We Gather Together" or "Danny Boy" while the new members are brought into the larger circle and their candles are lit.

Develop a "Choral Basics Catch-up" sheet to be mailed or handed out to new or less-experienced singers. It could include brief notes on such topics as what to expect, promptness, focus in rehearsals, how to mark music, and posture while singing.

CHOIR INTERVIEWS

Schedule once-a-year choir interviews (which may or may not be combined with mini–voice hearings). Start out by asking, "Is there anything I can do to make your choir experience better?" and "Is there any way in particular you feel you might serve the choir program?" This creates the sense that the choir is also theirs. When a person is included in the ownership, his or her motivation increases.

CHAPTER 28

BUILDING THE SUPPORT SYSTEM

PUTTING PARENTS IN THE LOOP

Keep in touch with the parents of your youth and children's choir members. Write, e-mail, or call the parents of at least two choir members a week, not about problems but about something good regarding their child. Keep a record of all such contacts in your roll book, and get around to everyone. There is always something to compliment. Include scheduling details, etc.

CHOIR WEBSITE

Consider establishing a website for your choir, especially as a vehicle to get information to parents. This provides the opportunity for parents to feel connected and in the know, without the need on your part to gather and process parental e-mail addresses. Perhaps it could be a link on your school or church's website. It could contain performance and rehearsal calendars, information about the music being worked on, trip information, and opportunities for parents and youth to help as volunteers. There could be a section about how rehearsals are going and your expectations for work outside of rehearsals. You could also include a list of the benefits of singing in a choir (see chapter 31). At the end of the page, put this attention-grabbing quote:

> There is a direct correlation between improved SAT scores and the length of time spent studying the arts. Those who studied the arts four or more years scored 59 points higher on verbal and 44 points higher on math portions of the SAT than students with no course work or experience in the arts.

> —"Profiles of SAT and Achievement Test Takers," The College Board, compiled by the MENC, 1995

CHOIR CHAT ROOM

Build relationships within your choir by setting up a choir online chat room, where members can share ideas about making the choir better and how members might support the choir and the director. This could be an excellent source of gaining feedback.

GATHERING WRITTEN FEEDBACK

Gather written feedback once, or perhaps twice, a year. Have a form that is easy to fill out on the chairs as choir members arrive and have extra pencils available. Take the first five minutes of rehearsal to have them write down one thing they really like about the choir and one suggestion for improvement of any kind. Signatures are optional, but may be helpful as you endeavor to follow up on the suggestions. Give singers your personal commitment not to be defensive . . . and to come back to them within three weeks with new ideas for the choir based on some of those suggestions. Reiterate the importance of their input in continually refining their choir. When they feel that they share ownership and a sense of vision with the director, they work harder as choir members.

TALK LESS AND LISTEN MORE

In conversations with choir members or colleagues, become a better listener. The most effective conversations are often those in which you talk less and listen more. Be wary of monopolizing conversations. When others are talking, don't let yourself interrupt. You will be able to tell when the other person's thoughts take a pause, and that's the time to jump in. When you are speaking, notice when others have something to say. When others are talking, instead of planning your next interjection, think about what they are saying and how they feel about it. Then use that as a basis for what you will say next. Occasionally summarize what they have just said to make sure you understand—and to let them know you value what they are saying.

CHOIR MEMBER BRAIN TRUST

Develop a brain trust of key choir members (and/or parents for student-age choirs) to keep you aware of the pulse of the choir, constantly evaluating how things are going and discussing fresh ideas. They should have short meetings at least quarterly. This also gives ownership to your leaders, who then have a vested interest in the success of the choir.

CHAPTER 29

MOTIVATING YOURSELF PAST PROBLEMS

ACTION, NOT WORRY!

Always a step to take. There is a solution to almost every problem—or at least some step you can take to begin turning things around. It may take a positive outlook and persistent imagination, but when you are faced with a problem, find some small step to take in a positive direction. The solution will come, but sometimes it's a journey, not an immediate breakthrough.

Meet problems head on. When the inevitable problems arise, meet them head on. They won't go away; they will, in fact, grow in their destructive capacity if left to simmer. Face-to-face dialogue as soon as possible usually provides the best opportunity for resolution. Give the other side the benefit of believing in their good intentions and ask the same of them toward you. Then listen—a lot—and try to understand the problem from the other's perspective.

Take little steps today. Problems never just sit there: they get bigger each day they are left untended. Soon those small annoyances have become huge and debilitating—at least in our minds. Stop right now and make a list of no more than five things over which you have been fretting. Under each problem write one or two small steps you can take, so that tomorrow the problem will be at least a little better than it is today. You don't have to solve the problems, only commit to taking small, positive steps. Soon the anguish factor begins to recede, and those accumulated small steps open the door to solutions. Action keeps the gremlins away.

PROBLEMS WITH INDIVIDUALS

Developing one-on-one relationships. Developing personal relationships with your singers is the key to motivating your choirs, especially when the relationship with the choir as a whole seems to have gone slack. There is nothing like one-on-one conversations to begin the building or rebuilding process. Start by setting up fifteen-minute interviews with every choir member.

The objectives are:
- to show you know and care about them as individuals
- to let them sense your commitment to do all you can to make choir a great experience for them
- to elicit at least one suggestion from them about anything having to do with the choir
- to ask their commitment to look for ways to make a positive contribution
- to say that your door is always open if they have any concerns or ideas that might benefit the choir during the year
- to sign them up for a twenty-minute mini–voice lesson during the next month or so, so that you can get to know their voice better

What to do with those troubled voices. Dale Carnegie once said, "When fates hands you a lemon, make lemonade." Instead of gritching about the problem voices or personalities in your choir, do something about it. For problem voices, have them come for an individual session with you. Even if you do not have extensive vocal background, listen carefully and see if you can imitate with your own voice what the problem is. Then work from there. The answer is usually "back to the basics": posture and head position, breath support, placement, and, especially, not overdoing it. Often problem voices are enthusiastic choir members who want to give their all. The need is usually to begin phrases with more finesse and less power. Keep in mind that one can see strain as easily as hear it, so look at them while they are singing for you. Nothing makes as significant a difference to choral sound as working with your singers individually early in the season.

Dealing with troublemakers. Do not let your choir's good morale be sidetracked by negative individuals. When inattention, side conversations, or negative comments begin to affect other choir members or you, appeal in private to the culprit's hidden nobility. "Jack, you have so much good in you, so much you could do in a positive way for this choir, how about putting the choir first? Do the right thing. Be all you can be." Watch him for any sign of improvement, and when it comes, in any way, acknowledge your appreciation to him in front of the choir. Let him be known for doing something well. Then after rehearsal, send him a letter or an e-mail, not about the original problem, but about how much it meant to you when he began to try his best.

Ask for his commitment to give more of the same next rehearsal. For someone who is used to getting yelled at, this feels good.

Give problem personalities a special job. Problem personalities usually just want to be noticed, so give them special responsibilities. Instead of fighting them, put them on your leadership team. Problem personalities are usually strong personalities; they will always make an impact of some kind. They are hard-wired that way. They don't have a choice. So put them in the position to make a positive impact and get public recognition for doing it. Give them a positive job. Put them in charge of shepherding new members, of drawing up a list of choir rules and traditions to give to new members, or ask them to have their radar up during the next few rehearsals for ideas on how to make rehearsals more efficient—any job that feeds their need to be noticed, but one which is positive and supportive of the choir and you. Have them bring suggestions to you, but only outside of rehearsals. Chances are that these will be helpful suggestions, and your expressions of gratitude will further enhance their new positive style.

Nip trouble in the bud. Confront troublemakers or people problems of any kind as soon as possible, preferably in person, or, at least, by phone. This takes courage and diplomacy, but it is worth the discomfort to reach an understanding.

Research their interests. When dealing with a difficult person, a choir member, colleague, committee member or administrative overseer, take the time to do some research. Find out about the person's special interests or hobbies, and read up on them. The next time you get the chance, strike up a conversation about this person's interests, instead of yours. Build the relationship first. The support will follow afterwards, and you will also be more of an enlightened person outside of your own field.

When apologies are due. Being a choir director is a people business, and sooner or later we all end up offending someone. Distance grows and the relationship becomes awkward. Communicate immediately with anyone you may have offended, no matter the circumstances, and offer apologies. You can explain your intentions after the apology, but you certainly didn't mean for them to be hurt, and that's the primary message. Express regret that hurtful things were said or mistakes made. Acknowledge the genuineness of the other person's feelings, and say that you would like to make the attempt to repair damage and understand the other person's viewpoint. Along the way, point out something positive about them that you appreciate or admire (there is always something). This often begins a conversation that is the first step toward reconciliation. It won't kill you, and it may well remove a tremendous weight from your soul and theirs.

Servant or slave? When experiencing some difficulties in working with your bosses, consider discussing with them the differences between being one's servant and being one's slave, as pointed out by M. Scott Peck in *Further along the Road Less Traveled.* A slave does what he or she is told, but a servant uses sensitivity and creativity to do what is in the best interest of the other. You would like to be free to use your creativity to enhance the job and support the vision of your boss.

Communicating with colleagues. Could you use some cooperation from choir members or colleagues? You can inspire cooperation by first giving some out. How might you be of service to them? Get inside their minds and see how you might reach out to them. Cooperation has a boomerang effect: What goes around, comes around.

BE WILLING TO CHANGE YOURSELF

Change yourself first. When there is a difficult problem that needs to be faced, see what steps you can take on your own before asking others to modify their behavior. The temptation is for us to point a finger at someone else, but putting all the blame and burden on others won't start you toward a solution. So first take several corrective steps yourself so others can see you have made a good-faith effort to go halfway. That creates an atmosphere conducive to working together toward a solution.

What do you choose to hear? If you find yourself discouraged with your rehearsals, it may have to do with what you choose to see and hear. In every circumstance, in everything your choir sings, some things are good and others are less so. What we are after is a balance, but we must begin with what is right, not what is wrong. If we as conductors become overwhelmed with all the things that are wrong, and then enumerate them to our choirs, both conductor and singers will be discouraged. So, early in the rehearsal, let the choir sing a bit without interruption while you use your listening skills to hear both what is good and what needs attention. Then give the choir a few good strokes before pointing out no more than a couple of other skills or sensitivities that need some attention. Everyone is more motivated, including you.

Lose your troubles in others. The truth is that there are times when we get discouraged. A sense of personal depression sets in, and we can't help dwelling on how badly things are going for us. Try losing your troubles in others. Reach out to someone else who is struggling, perhaps a choir member or a colleague, and do all you can to help him or her through their troubles. You will have made a difference in someone else's life, and you will come away with a renewed sense of self-worth and respect for yourself.

Hang in there! When you are going though a rough period, have faith and hang in there! If you love what you do, give selflessly of yourself, genuinely care for the people you work with, and do what you can to see things from the perspectives of others, and you *will* find your way. Either things will turn around for the better or another door will open for you. If the latter happens, you will be able to embrace new opportunities without the baggage of bitterness.

Avoid negative conversations. Avoid getting sucked into negative conversations about people. Such conversations end up deepening animosity that you should be working to overcome. The other danger is that these negative conversations have a way of getting back to the people concerned.

KEEPING THE HIGHS AND LOWS IN PERSPECTIVE

See criticism as an opportunity for growth. Develop the capacity to respond to criticism positively, looking at it as an opportunity for growth. Almost all criticism has a seed of truth in it, at least from the perspective of the person providing it. Two responses are helpful: How can I use this information to get better at something, and, from these comments, what can I learn about how to work with this person? Any discussion should be to clarify the concern, but avoid defending or explaining yourself. Rather, thank the person for the helpful food for thought.

Set aside bruised feelings. Sometimes you have to set aside bruised feelings in order to create an atmosphere conducive to healing. When we have been wounded—and this is particularly true of artists—our bitterness becomes entrenched. Then we can hardly think about the other person, much less have a productive conversation. If you want to regain peace in your professional life, whether with a choir member or a colleague, be the better person. Look to the better good that could come of taking small steps toward reconciliation. A "lose-lose" becomes a "win-win."

When you need a safe place. When you find yourself in a particularly difficult situation where you are close to reacting in a way beneath your best person and not in your best interests, step away mentally for a moment by singing in your mind a phrase or two from a meaningful piece of music. My escape mantra is from Jane Marshall's setting of the poem "Prayer for Hard Things" by Edith Kent Battle. "There are hard things that I must do today, dear God. Hard things, and I should like to do them well, and bravely as I can. I ask for courage." I can't tell you how many times this piece that I learned as a child has helped me keep my cool in tough moments. This method is a safety net that allows you to face potentially difficult situations with grace and a calm demeanor. You are still in the meeting and still looking and listening, but your soul is at peace.

Reacting to compliments. The successes that we have as choir directors are highly visible, and we tend to receive many compliments. But the truth is that many people are part of our successes, so spread the credit around. Multiply every compliment by immediately sharing the spotlight with the entire choir, the choir officers, and your colleagues on the staff. You will have lost nothing, and their dedication to and support of you will only continue to grow. So when compliments come, be gracious, but don't let them go to your head. We should absolutely be thrilled with each success, but let others talk about it. People who beat their chests and look with disdain upon others of lesser talent are generally disliked, and their own artistic sensitivity declines. Better to concentrate more on others than yourself, and on creating and sharing beauty.

Learning from disappointments. Turn the tables on disappointment. Rather than letting the school of hard knocks defeat you, search out what you can learn from these unfortunate experiences and get busy doing something about them. Treat every disappointment as a wake-up call, an opportunity for growth. If your choirs got hammered for their tuning in a contest, be grateful for the nudge and work on that skill for next year. If you didn't get accepted into an auditioned workshop chorus, sign up for some voice lessons. Napoleon Hill said that "every adversity has the seed of an equivalent or greater benefit" (*Success through a Positive Mental Attitude*), so face disappointments with courage and fortitude, and let them make you better. The worse your situation, the more spectacular the rebound!

Compliment in public; criticize in person. Give compliments in public, in letters or e-mails, but when it is necessary to criticize or deal with problems, do so privately in person. Above all, never handle delicate problems by e-mail. There is no way to clarify your intentions; there is a substantial chance of being misunderstood; and there is a tendency to burn bridges from the safety of distance, which you will often later regret.

Learning from mistakes. Don't dwell on your mistakes. Learn from them. Analyze what led to the mistake, what you might have done to prevent it, and how to avoid it in the future. Then make that adjustment in your thinking and methodology.

CHAPTER 30

ADOPTING A NEW PERSPECTIVE

SENSING HOW THE OTHER PERSON FEELS

Imagine yourself in the place of others, and try to see things from their perspective. How do they perceive you? What can you do to make that perception more positive and welcoming? What does the rehearsal room look and feel like to a singer, rather than to the conductor? Every part of both rehearsals and personal relationships would benefit from imagining how things feel to others. Too often, we slip into problems by concentrating too much on what *we* feel like, or how *we* think rehearsal is going. But it's not about us; it's about our singers, our colleagues, the parents of our students, and our bosses, and how they perceive the programs and choirs that we run. Mentally look at things from their perspectives.

What does the singer see? What does the rehearsal room look like to the singers? All that clutter behind you when you conduct doesn't bother you, but it may be frenetic to them. What about the lighting of the room, the color of the paint, or the room temperature? How clear are your gestures to them (you won't know this until you have someone videotape you during a rehearsal)? How much do you talk compared to how much the group actually sings? When those whom you teach or with whom you work sense that you try to see things from their perspectives, motivation increases.

Become an actor. Take a page out of the Stanislavsky acting method. It says that before you play the part of a plumber, actually take a job as a plumber, so that you identify completely with that character. We can do that, too, in a sense. When you are talking with someone, try to stand in that person's shoes and comprehend why they are saying what they are saying. This often allows you to grasp solutions more quickly. Conversations are opportunities to understand others. They should rarely be about you.

Assume others' good intentions. Make it your new default reaction in working with choir members, colleagues, committee members, and administrational supervisors to assume their good intentions. Strive to see the good intentions of others. Almost everybody believes him- or herself to be a good person. If we can learn to look at problems from the other's perspective and be sensitive to that, almost all problems can be worked out.

Adjust to peculiarities. Adjust how you deal with the peculiarities and personal styles of others. We all have tendencies or traits—some innate, some environmental. We come to decisions from different perspectives. Different things are important to us, e.g., for some of us, the final result is all-important; but for others, following correct procedures is more important than the result. You will communicate more efficiently and get along more peacefully by being sensitive to others' personal styles. Before significant conversations, take a moment to look at things from others' perspectives.

Are they really listening? Notice if choir members really listen to you. That's different from hearing. As a result of mega-marketing, people tune out most of what they hear. They have to choose to listen carefully. How can you tell if choir members are really tuned in . . . listening carefully? Look at them when you talk and when you conduct. Memorize at least some parts of most anthems, and use the intensity of your eyes to hold their attention.

EFFICIENCY

Are we doing too much? Many of our choral programs have more quantity than quality. We have so much to oversee that we can't do everything well. Are all those facets of the program necessary? Have any outlived their significance? Has your interest in some areas waned while you don't have enough time in areas of your greatest interest? Consider downsizing so that you can go deeper into activities that really matter to you and the institution.

The big picture. Start your day looking at the big picture. First thing each morning, before you get overwhelmed with that bulging to-do list, ask yourself what is going well with your life . . . and your choir. Write it down so you really acknowledge things about which you should be pleased. The tasks you need to do that day thus become vehicles for adding to something that is already going well. This approach accents present and future accomplishment, rather than leaving you feeling overwhelmed by that huge list of things you haven't done.

To-do lists. Choir directors usually have more to do than they can possibly get done. As a result, we flit from half-finished project to half-finished project, or, worse still, we become overwhelmed and give up completely. When faced with the quantity of a to-do list, prioritize. Some things absolutely have to get done, but some things that want your attention now are not important in the big picture. Some important things are not urgent, but cannot be put off for long. So decide carefully what goes to the top of your to do list for each day, and try to drop a few urgent but less important items completely. Also avoid time-consuming perfectionism where it is not beneficial in the big picture. Then concentrate on one task at a time.

One slice at a time. When a task is so large or complex that we don't know where to start, we tend to put off doing anything about it—except worry. Slice the job up into many smaller jobs and get one or two of those slices accomplished at a time. The key to keeping motivated is to take some action in the right direction. If you have a choir tour to plan, your first "slice" might be to start the process for finding venues. For church choirs, you might call Choristers Guild to find contacts in a projected area, or for schools, check the Internet for colleges or high schools that are known for having progressive music departments. That gets you started, and you can feel good about what you did today and take on another slice tomorrow.

Celebrate finished tasks. So often people who are trying to get back on track develop long lists of things to do. The problem is that such a list is overwhelming; no matter how much we get accomplished, the remaining list tends to destroy our momentum. The solution is to celebrate finished tasks. As you finish a job, move it to the top of a "done" list along with the date finished. Before wrapping up each day, take a moment to look over that growing track record of accomplishments and put yourself back on track.

MOTIVATING YOURSELF AND OTHERS: THE KEY TO SUCCESS

The salient message of part 3 is that we choir directors need to do all we can to stimulate success, to care for ourselves and our choir members with sensitivity and dignity, and to work our way positively through whatever problems arise. Following these steps to effective motivating should open the door to a higher level of fulfillment and enjoyment for you as a choir director. It should help you find your way past problems with choir members, developing a supportive team spirit within your choirs that makes your job easier. It should help you get yourself out of occasional ruts and back on track, sharing and experiencing the beauty and inspiration of music. It should increase your joy and sense of fulfillment in this marvelous gift of teaching others to sing, a gift that lasts a lifetime.

PART IV

GUARANTEED CHOIR RECRUITING

INTRODUCTION: THE QUEST FOR MORE SINGERS

Most of us remember our first rehearsal as a conductor all too well. In my case, that rehearsal was for my first church choir, for which, as I recall, I had prepared thoroughly. I had studied the music, delved into the deeper meaning of the texts, and read up on related historical styles of interpretation. I had planned enticing warm-ups and carefully plotted how to begin to develop tone color, tuning, blend, dynamics, proportions, rhythmic accuracy, phrasing, and dramatic conviction. I had visions of grandeur as I waited in anticipation of the arrival of what was sure to be a glorious choir . . . which is not at all what walked in the door.

What did walk in were seven ladies and two men, most with significant vocal concerns, the majority being older singers well past their prime. What to do? Certainly, there were practical steps I could take to begin to work through their vocal problems, but that had little to do with my visions of grandeur and artistic hopes. I knew right then that nothing I could do would transform those singers into the choir of my dreams. Therefore, there were only two choices: either resign myself to scaling back my expectations or find a way to recruit more singers.

It's a fact to which we need to own up. In most church choirs and community choruses, the average age of members has increased dramatically. The old members keep getting older until they finally retire from the choir, and there are precious few younger singers willing to take their places. Young adults today lead ever more hectic lives, and the once-natural tendency of those who sang in high school or college choirs to continue singing in adult choirs has faded. Concerns for enough choir members are evident in younger choirs too. High schoolers who loved to sing as children are drawn elsewhere by myriad enticing activities.

Adult and youth choirs are not filling up on their own any more, and it is time that we choir directors wake up and learn to become proactive in building our choirs. That is what is so different about what we do as compared to instrumental performers. If instrumentalists study hard and practice diligently, they have just to take out their instruments to be able to make satisfying music. Choir directors, on the other hand, add to their artistic preparation the necessity of building their own instrument—the choir. Finding and recruiting singers is the first step, followed by developing the choir's sound, teaching them to be artistic, and motivating them to give their best. But nothing of substance can be achieved until you recruit enough singers to have a viable choir.

Is finding more singers impossible where you are? I don't believe it. Choir membership can be increased dramatically in almost every situation. Over the years I have found myself in several situations where the choirs were either in serious decline or nonexistent. Instead of letting the low numbers get me down, I was determined to learn to recruit. As a result of what I learned, I eventually was able to build from ground level two high school choral programs, four church youth choirs, two adult community choruses, and one adult community symphony orchestra, in addition to revitalizing several adult church choirs.

Part 4 offers insights and step-by-step procedures for recruiting choir members that I developed in the process of building all those programs. There is much more to this process than an announcement of the first rehearsal and a general invitation to "come on out." For instance, taking the time to develop goals—what is important about singing in choirs—gives depth and purpose to your recruiting. Then finding ways to market those goals builds a natural support system, so that lots of others are helping you recruit. It also stimulates curiosity about the choirs, making the choirs the "talk in the halls." Then comes the important process of gathering names of prospective choir members, using slightly different procedures according to the ages of the choirs involved.

These and a wealth of other techniques for the actual recruiting process are all included in part 4. It shows you how to make recruiting not only successful, but also a delightful experience for all those involved and a pervasive stimulus to the broader institution and the community at large. These chapters demonstrate how, throughout the entire recruiting process, unstoppable enthusiasm must become your default attitude, flinging wide the doors to larger, healthier choirs and, eventually, the artistic fulfillment we so desire.

If you find yourself with a lemon of a choir program, part 4 shows you how to make lemonade!

CHAPTER 31

DEVELOPING WORTHY GOALS

As an example of how we might be proactive in recruiting, let's briefly consider recruiting specifically for a youth choir. The philosophy and procedures are similar for choirs of any age.

When I interviewed for my first job as a church choir director, I was told the chances of building a successful youth choir were slim to none. There was no tradition on which to build, and no one seemed to think it was remotely possible. Parents felt their youth were overcommitted, and many saw a youth choir as one more social activity without redeeming value. Why should they urge, or even allow, their children to participate? The budget committee was leery of providing necessary funds for an unknown, unproven activity. The recurring question was, What is it about the choir experience that warrants our support?

The only answer I could come up with at the moment was that many schools and churches have youth choirs, and besides, that's what I was hired to do. The committee made it clear that my response was not good enough. I was to come back to them when I could convince them of the importance of this new choir. What's in it for the singers and for us? When I could tell them that, they would come up with the support and budget needed . . . but not before! They wanted to know specifically how a good choir program would benefit the youth involved and the church community.

Knowing that it would be impossible to build a healthy program without the active support of the budget committee and parents, I spent the next several weeks coming up with the necessary ammunition, a philosophical statement of the value of the choirs. I started by asking several veteran choir directors how they would have answered the budget committee's question. Soon I had a strong list of the benefits of a youth choir, both for the singers and the church (for your purposes, this may be the school).

Lists such as these are powerful tools for both recruiting and building support for your choir program. Take a careful look at my lists and add your own ideas. Your "Why Bother with

Choirs" lists will vary according to the nature of the choir you are building—e.g., for adults, for youth or children, for school, for church or community—but having this philosophical reasoning will be a significant asset in gaining support where it counts, which is the first step of successful recruiting.

WHY BOTHER WITH CHOIRS: HOW THEY BENEFIT THE SINGERS

Singing in a choir . . .

1. is an easy way to make lots of new friends and feel a part of the group.
2. can become a "hook" in the college application process, showing well-balanced experience and education, which includes cultural sophistication.
3. develops youths' and children's sense of culture and sophistication.
4. is therapeutic; rehearsals become a time when singers can put aside, for a while at least, the other pressures and concerns of the day.
5. develops poise under pressure.
6. teaches beneficial posture and breathing techniques.
7. helps develop better enunciation.
8. shows the positive, exciting impact a cohesive group can make beyond that which is possible for an individual.
9. teaches the value of careful preparation in reaching goals.
10. teaches that there are no short cuts to excellence.
11. shows the singers that their leadership, demeanor, and good attitude make a significant contribution to the success of the group.
12. teaches a sense of responsibility and how to set priorities.
13. gives members a sense of pride and self-worth.
14. provides the foundation for a lifetime of enjoyment in music.
15. trains participants to be future supporters of the arts.
16. provides musical memories that can take you momentarily out of difficult situations by calling to mind a beautiful piece of music.
17. opens the door to wonderful poetry in a medium easy to recall many years later.
18. teaches an historical perspective through music and texts conceived during different periods of history.

Further, singing specifically in a church choir . . .

19. serves as an effective vehicle for teaching the faith, especially to children and youth. We learn almost as much of our faith through the texts of the hymns and anthems we sing as from sermons or lectures. Children sing before they learn to read—or listen to sermons.

20. enables one to serve in one of the ministries of the worshiping community.
21. provides an anchor for regular church participation at a time when secular attractions and pressures pull many away from church participation.

The previous list of the benefits of singing in a choir deals specifically with positive effects on the participating singers. These arguments are helpful in gaining the trust and support of parents, as well as school administrators or church leaders. Moreover, this list can be a vital tool in recruiting adults when asking prospects to devote one night each week to singing in a choir, and for many, a few hours more on the weekend.

A word of caution: Many of these philosophical benefits of singing in choir are not useful in direct conversations with the youth and children. Although young singers will undoubtedly benefit in these ways, their reasons for joining a choir (your means of enticing them) are usually less high-minded. So, consider their perspective in deciding how to entice them. The important thing is to get them into the choir, and only then do you have the opportunity to make a difference in their lives.

Now that you have developed a list of philosophical benefits for the choir members, how do you gain the support of those cautious decision makers and budget controllers who may not share the same perspective of the parents and singers, and may not be ardent supporters of the arts? What's in it for them? How, they may ask, would a healthy choir program benefit the church, school, or community? Again, here is my list, to which you should add benefits unique to your situation and organization.

WHY BOTHER WITH CHOIRS: HOW THEY BENEFIT THE CHURCH, SCHOOL, OR ORGANIZATION

A healthy choir program . . .
1. can be a catalyst for excitement and promotion within the organization.
2. can provide musical leadership and beauty to all important ceremonies of the organization:

Schools
- Flag-raising ceremonies
- Holiday programs
- Fund-raising events
- Awards banquets
- Community service functions
- High-profile sporting events
- Graduation ceremonies

Churches
- Virtually all worship services
- Installation of ministers
- Significant liturgical festival celebrations
- Stewardship campaigns
- Fund-raising events
- Mission fairs
- Memorial services

3. can become an extension of almost every facet of the organization by finding some way of supporting its causes.
4. can draw in family and friends of the singers within the walls of the institution, where their support of the larger institution might be cultivated.
5. can become one of the more visible arms of the organization, and the positive image they portray creates strong public relations.

Now you can answer the question "Why bother with choirs?" When you seek support for the choir program, naysayers will now realize that your effort will make a positive impact on the lives of the singers. In addition, you can show that the choir program can strengthen and support the larger organization in many important ways.

CHAPTER 32

MARKETING YOUR PHILOSOPHY

Now that you have developed your own lists of the benefits of singing, how do you use this information? Start by printing the "Why Bother with Choirs" lists on an attractive, eye-catching information sheet. Make lots of copies, because you are going to distribute them to all the people and groups who could help you get the recruiting ball rolling.

Who are these potential supporters, and how might one encourage that endorsement? Below are listed the kinds of people who have been helpful to me in building past programs in schools and churches. Add to these your own ideas of influential leaders in your organization whose support would surely be an asset.

POTENTIAL SUPPORTER CATEGORIES FOR SCHOOLS AND CHURCHES

- Administrative heads (principals and headmasters, senior ministers, committee chairs—the people with authority)
- Business managers
- Development, stewardship, or evangelism chairs
- Other music teachers, organists, and colleagues in the arts
- Notable retired teachers, administrators, ministers, and former music directors who still have strong contacts at the institution
- Frustrated singers or parents
- Historically antimusic people

OTHER POTENTIAL SUPPORTER CATEGORIES SPECIFICALLY FOR SCHOOLS

- Chairs of parents' support organizations
- Deans and counselors (especially those who advise students on course selections)
- Respected teachers in unrelated disciplines or departments (e.g., drama, history, English, foreign-language)
- Sports coaches

OTHER POTENTIAL SUPPORTER CATEGORIES SPECIFICALLY FOR CHURCHES

- Ministers
- Christian educators and youth ministers
- Lay volunteers in other ministries
- Worship committee chairs
- Mission/Outreach chairs
- Secretarial staff
- Leaders of the church-sponsored scouting troop(s)
- Choral and instrumental directors in nearby high schools and/or colleges

Some of these categories inevitably will not apply to your situation, but search out those that do make sense for you, adding any other useful ones. Don't disregard those people who might see a strong choir program as unwanted competition to their own areas of interest. The intention is that you reach out to the movers and shakers of your own institution, the people who set the tone for most of what goes on. Those are the names that need to end up on this list, even if you don't sense their support at present. Most institutions are replete with people and groups seeking support for themselves. Some of these may see music as a potential drain on their own support and popularity. The cloud of doubt hanging over an energetic new program can fester into unhealthy competition and backbiting. With enough sensitivity and care, it is possible to gain almost anyone's support. Once people sense your openness toward them and your genuine interest in being a positive influence, it is natural that they would then feel supportive of your efforts. Turn institutional leaders your way by valuing them and what they believe in . . . before building up your own turf.

To avoid any possible sense of competition and to gain the support of these successful people, you must communicate your goals. Although such people may not seem supportive and may even send negative vibrations at first, be proactive in opening positive lines of communication with them. Think of ways in which the choirs might support their programs or interests. Support is a two-way street, and support offered has a way of coming back when you need it most.

Now that you have a specific list of those you would like to see in your support system, it's time to get their attention, to let them know about your goals and to let them see the potential advantage of your program to their own interests. It is time to set up meetings and prepare for those interviews.

CHAPTER 33

TIPS FOR INTERVIEWS WITH POTENTIAL SUPPORTERS

A DIGRESSION ABOUT CHARMING NOTES

How does one go about making effective personal contacts with those whom you wish to recruit and those whose support you seek? In her marvelous book *Making a Literary Life* (Random House, 2002), author Carolyn See includes an intriguing chapter about writing "charming notes." She makes the point that building relationships with people that are important to you is like dating. In a sense, it is a matter of "courtship and wooing, flirting and chatting." She strongly suggests that we write at least one "charming note" a day . . . for the rest of our lives. What would sending out such notes accomplish? They leave the recipient with a wonderful sense of being noticed and admired. They give a satisfying sense of self-worth. They elicit responses, creating the impetus for a relationship.

Carolyn See's "charming notes" are written on half-sheet stationary as expensive or cheap as you like, with matching smaller envelopes if possible. The investment in slightly higher-quality stationary with your name on the envelope and your e-mail address in small type at the bottom of the letter page will increase the sense that these notes are significant and that you genuinely value the recipients. Start your note by saying something charming and genuine about the person, about their talent or their contributions to the institution or the choir. Then, if they don't know you personally, explain who you are and what you do. Finally, convey to them that it would mean much to you to get to know them better in the future. Thank them again for their contributions or congratulate them on their accomplishments. The entire hand-written note should run between four and six sentences, an elegant and charming icebreaker for the personal contacts that follow. Charming notes are also powerful motivators to current choir members, well worth sending several after every rehearsal.

THE FIRST CONTACT: SETTING UP THE MEETINGS

Begin by sending each person on your potential supporters list a copy of your "Why Bother with Choirs" philosophical sheet. Add a "charming note" saying how much you would appreciate meeting with them to gather input about how the choir program is perceived. Explain that you are going through a process of a "choir makeover" before the new season begins, that you would value their thoughts about the choir program in the past, and appreciate their reaction to your ideas for the future.

Applaud their efforts on behalf of the institution and their sensitivity to the pulse of the institution. Because of the uniqueness of those contributions, you are asking to benefit from their gained insights. Sharing a few moments of their time in the next week or so is an opportunity for them to be heard and to make a significant impact on what the future choir program will look like. Don't ask overtly for their support—you want their perspective on how the choir program can best function within the broader context and goals of the institution. Once they have had the opportunity to share their input, such support will often follow naturally, but the purpose of the meetings must be your genuine interest in understanding their point of view.

For any soon-to-be supporters who do not work within your school or church office complex, offer to meet them near their own place of business, perhaps for lunch at a time convenient to you both. This effort on your part shows them that you are serious about this meeting and that you value their input.

PREPARING FOR THE MEETINGS

In preparation for meetings with potential supporters, think creatively about *their* areas, searching out ways in which the choir program could support *them*. Plan to bring up those ideas and get their reaction. Whether or not they accept your specific suggestions for this mutual support, the idea of cooperation has been planted. You want them to see you and the choir program as an asset. They now know that you are supportive of them and want to work cohesively with them.

When the meeting begins, be friendly and assure them you know they are busy and their time is valuable. Offer your support of their area(s) and express your desire to eventually earn theirs. Ask about their hopes and dreams for their work within the institution. Discuss possible ways in which you and the choir program could show its support for their hopes and dreams. Then ask if they received your "Why Bother" sheet. If not, give them a new copy. After allowing some time for them to glance through it, ask for their reactions. Emphasize that the choir program is not about *you*, but rather, is about doing something positive for the singers and for the institution. Part of your choir program's success depends upon input from significant leaders like them, and that requires their understanding of what your goals for the program are. Ask them if they would be willing to do two specific things: (1) name one good thing about the choir program in the past, and (2) make one suggestion of how it might improve in some way, or some aspect that needs attention.

During the meeting, take careful notes, asking for clarifications as needed. Avoid getting on your own soapbox, thereby monopolizing the conversation. Let them do most the talking. In the business world, it is generally recognized that interviewees (in this case, potential supporters) are most impressed with interviews in which they had the opportunity to give input more than listen to someone else talk. Your listening skills make the interviewee feel important, valued, and heard and help you see the choir program in a larger context.

As the meeting comes to a close, summarize the main points of your discussion for accuracy. Then ask for some time to consider their suggestions or comments. Set a date, maybe about three weeks after the meeting, when you will meet with them again or write them a letter or an e-mail detailing specific steps you plan to take in response to their input.

The bottom line is that going through this careful process of gathering input from significant people related to your institution gains their respect and provides you with stimulating food for thought. It is also likely that they will have good things to say about you and the choir program in their own spheres of influence.

THINGS TO DISCUSS WITH SPECIFIC INTERVIEWEES

Let's take a few moments to consider some particular topics and approaches when meeting with specific interviewees.

Administrative heads (principals and headmasters, senior ministers, committee chairs):
- Describe your initial recruiting procedures.
- Ask if they would be willing to say a short word on behalf of the choir program's recruiting efforts in some public way to help get things up and running; one brief statement from them is worth ten from you. (This also conveys to them your sense of their importance and value.)
- Set up another meeting in three months to update your progress in building up the program.

Business managers:
- Ask when budgets are due and about how you could help develop a tighter, more accurate music budget.
- Ask for clarifications on purchasing procedures and time needed to respond to budgetary requests, as well as the type of record keeping that would be helpful to them.
- Ask how budgets are reconciled at the end of the fiscal year and what you could do to make that procedure more efficient.
- Ask if there are any other steps you could take to make the choir program more effective in budgeting and purchasing.
- Reassure them that you will respond to any financial concern immediately, and mention you would appreciate their support of the choir program.

Development, stewardship, evangelism chairs:
- Talk about the second half of your "Why Bother" sheet, which details the ways a strong choir program could benefit the institution.
- Express your understanding of the importance of fund-raising and marketing a positive image for the school or church.
- Ask about the major fund-raising events of the coming year and offer the choir's support.
- Discuss ways to get more members of the singers' families and the community at large out to choir events, and how to gather their names at those events for other possible avenues of support.

Colleagues in your own department (other music teachers, organists, etc.):
- Ask about the most difficult or frustrating aspect about their responsibilities and if there is any way you could help.
- Ask if there are any practical problems with how your areas relate that you might work on together.
- Set up an open-door policy in case either of you unintentionally does something to negatively impact the other's program. Always assuming good intentions on the other's part, agree to immediately discuss problems and how to avoid similar frustrations in the future.
- Discuss ways in which you or your choir could be of support during the coming year, projecting to others a sign of good feelings between your areas of primary concern.
- Express your ongoing support of their work and your desire to work together well. Again, it doesn't really matter if you haven't felt their support in the past. The expression of mutual support is the first step in achieving such cooperation.

Respected ministers or lay volunteers, and teachers in unrelated disciplines or departments:
- Compliment them on the good things others say about them.
- Tell them your hope is to create a similar, beneficial impact in your area.
- Ask if there are ways the choirs could support their special areas of interest, e.g., a special project that might benefit from having the choir sing.
- Tell them you would value any suggestions they have to help you "grow" the choir program in a positive way and to build the image of the choir.
- Suggest the benefits of letting others see your mutual respect and support.

Notable retired teachers, administrators, ministers, or former choir directors who still have strong contacts within the institution:
- Ask them about what they see as the most significant attributes of the choir program in the past, and if they would make one suggestion on how the current program might improve.
- Ask for ideas on recruiting and who in the institution might be helpful in this process.
- Express your appreciation of their support as you try to make a positive difference through the choir program.

Frustrated singers or parents:
- Thank them for caring enough about the choir program to want to see it be as good as it can be.
- Assure them you believe their intentions are good; say that you hope they believe the same about you.
- With that in mind, commit to them that you want to make things better. You cannot undo the past, but you are trying hard to take positive steps for the future.
- Ask if they are willing to help you find solutions that would make the choir program better; agree upon a first step that you could take together.
- Discuss what a positive signal it would send to other singers and parents if they became more involved and helped form a new, positive future.

Historically antimusic leaders in the institution (professional or volunteer):
- Use the same approach as under "Frustrated singers and parents," but also share the "Why Bother" sheets.
- Do a little research: find out what their nonmusical interests are. Read up on the subject (a basic online encyclopedia is a good place to start) and then look for an opportunity to

engage them in related conversation. They will find you more interesting and accessible, and this will open the door to other candid discussions involving the choir program.

- Say that you understand that they haven't always been pleased with the choir program and that you would value their input on ways to create a better program.
- Take careful notes. At the end of the meeting, ask to review your notes together for accuracy. Say that you will be back in touch with them within three weeks with specific steps you are taking in response to their input.
- Explain what a difference it would make if they would let others know of your intention to do all you can to improve the choir program.

IDEAS SPECIFICALLY CONCERNING SCHOOLS

Chairs of parents' support organizations:
- Ask about major parents' committee functions during the year and whether the choir(s) might be of assistance.
- Offer to include a note from the their committee with your letter to the parents of choir members at the beginning of the school year, and ask whether you might do the same in *their* mailing.
- Invite them to say a few words about the work of their committee during the first choir concert of the year, at which uninvolved parents might be in attendance.
- Emphasize the difference it would make if members of their committee were to actively support the choir on a regular basis.

Deans, advisors and counselors (especially those who advise students on course selections):
- Discuss what a positive experience a good choral program can be for students, especially in offering a balance to what colleges see in transcripts by portraying a well-rounded person, and providing an opportunity for students to use their talents in service to both the school and the broader community.
- Give them a list of students who either have musical background and experience, or have performed well in the younger choirs of the school (see chapter 35). Request that the option of joining choir be made directly to those students during the course selection process.
- Offer to have choral ensembles from the choir sing for feeder schools or at any other venue where the institution could benefit from such a positive public image.

- Invite the development (fund-raising) department or committee to host a reception at major choir events, including alumni receptions after out-of-town concerts.

Drama teachers:
- Let them know that you will encourage your choir members to sign up for drama classes and to audition for the annual school musical, because acting enhances the choral experience.
- Elaborate on the idea that your two departments should be seen as related, supportive arts and that students from each discipline would benefit from exposure to the other.
- Offer your assistance with drama productions, e.g., help the actor-singers learn their notes or provide vocal coaching on an "as needed" basis.
- Invite the drama teacher to give a short talk to the choirs about mood and dramatic energy when in performance.
- If the performance space is shared, discuss the scheduling needs of both departments. Work through any necessary "give and take," asking at what times of the year the drama students are under the most pressure—and therefore promising to limit the choir pressure at that time—and vice versa.
- Discuss the benefits of positive comments you both could make to your respective ensembles and potential supporters about each other's programs.

History teachers:
- Ask if they would be willing to help by clarifying for you historical allusions in the season's music, or about what life was like at the time when more historical music or texts were written.
- Discuss the possibility of designing a concert using folk music or historical pieces with a narration giving an historical perspective of those times, perhaps with their involvement as narrator.
- Once your music (and the texts) has been chosen for the year, ask if you might provide them with a copy, with the hope they might alert you to related classes you might sit in on.
- Encourage them to talk up the choir should the opportunity present itself—and assure them of the choir's appreciation "in advance."

English teachers:
- Reflect with them how the composition of choral music begins with a carefully chosen text and only a blank sheet of manuscript paper. The text defines the shape and feel of the composition for which it is the inspiration. A study and

understanding of the texts is the natural starting place in a conductor's preparation, and a discussion of the text with the choir members is a significant part of any choral rehearsal.

- Ask for their assistance in your proper understanding of complex texts, e.g., Robert Frost's poetry in Randall Thompson's "Frostiana."
- Sound out whether they would be interested in providing an introduction to the poetry before the choir presents such music in an upcoming concert?
- Inquire if they would like to see the more interesting texts of choral pieces for the next season ahead of time, in case there was the possibility of interdepartmental cooperative teaching. In this way, you hope that they might see the choral department as an asset to, and perhaps even an extension of, the English department.
- Say how much it would mean to your growing program to have their public support.

Foreign-language teachers:
- To show that you are interested in their area of expertise, schedule some foreign-language repertoire during the year and ask for their help with correct pronunciation in advance.
- Show them a list of your students and ask which are enrolled in foreign-language courses, with the hope that some of these students might be able to help you teach pronunciation of foreign song texts to the choir.
- Ask them if they would be willing to check provided translations for accuracy during the course of the year and perhaps to assist you with word-for-word translations to understand the proper interpretation of the musical ideas in relationship to the texts.
- Ask if you could sit in on a few classes to get a better feel for the language you will be teaching the choir.
- Ask if they would be interested in having some choir members perform various foreign-language pieces for their language classes during the year.
- Suggest what a difference it would make if they would talk up the choir were that opportunity to present itself.

Sports coaches:
- Ask for a schedule of major sports events for the coming season. Say that you will get to as many events as you can and that you will encourage choir members to support the teams.
- Point out the physical similarities between playing sports and singing in a choir. (See the list of sports analogies in chapter 24.)

- Reflect on the similarities between coaching and choir directing, e.g., recruiting talent, motivating for success, developing teamwork, technical training, and teaching the ability to adjust, think, see, and hear.
- Ask if they would be willing to come talk to the choir about the importance of physical training to a healthy life and to offer some suggestions for starting a personal exercise routine.
- Offer to provide some singers for the national anthem before important games or matches.
- Say what a difference it would make to feel their support for the choral program.

IDEAS SPECIFICALLY CONCERNING CHURCHES

Ministers:
- Make it clear to him or her that you see the music department as an extension of their vision, their hopes and dreams, for the church community. Before you develop the plans for a new season, you want to make sure you understand what is important to them and use it as a basis for your own planning.
- Say that you would like to spend some time thinking about that vision and then come back in another week with several suggestions on how the music department might be able to help the church move in that direction.
- Remember that ministers often have baggage from dealing with musicians who insisted upon going their own way and never had such a discussion with the ministers about sharing their hopes and dreams for the church. Don't react negatively to what you see as subtle negative indicators, knowing that you have to win his or her confidence by your future actions and continued awareness of the broader issues of the church.
- Avoid talking initially about your exciting plans for the choir program. That discussion can wait for the next time, after you have demonstrated your interest in the vision of the minister in charge. Then your own plans are seen as coming under the theological and philosophical umbrella of sensitivity to the broader church.

Christian Educators and Youth Ministers:
- Tell them your priority is the youth and children whom you are both called to serve and that music is a tool to help them grow in faith and in their relationships with one another. With that in mind, discuss how you can join efforts to benefit the children and youth (not you).

- Suggest ways you might be visibly supportive of one another's programs so that the participants and their parents sense teamwork, expressing your shared hope that the youth and children participate in both the Christian education and the music programs.
- Ask if, during the early part of the year, you might each have the opportunity to make announcements and extend invitations during each other's activities.
- Discuss chaperoning each other's activities and trips. These are good opportunities to get to know kids who are not currently involved in both programs.
- Set up a regular chat time early in the week to discuss how the past weekend's activities went for each of you. Are there any concerns about which you should both be aware? Are there any kids that seem fragile or in danger of serious problems?

Lay volunteers in other ministries:
- The object of this meeting is to get to know each other. It is not about the music department or what you hope to achieve. This conversation needs to be about them, what they do for the church, and how they go about it. What is it about their activities that means enough to them to be willing to volunteer?
- Compliment them on their commitment and the generosity of the time they give to the church.
- Ask if there is there anything that the music department can do to assist them in their ministries.
- Ask if there are any problem areas between the music department and their ministries and what suggestions they may have to improve the situation or communication.
- Is there any way that they in their volunteer capacity could help the music department, e.g., urging others who might enjoy singing to consider joining choir?

Worship committee chairs:
- Depending on the church or denomination, this could be the same person as the music committee chair, but make sure they understand you want to use music to serve worship, not the other way around.
- Ask for their opinion of at least one thing that the music department does particularly well in worship; then ask for a suggestion of something you might try to improve. Agree to report back to them about what steps you will take in that regard.
- Discuss ways in which music could make the service smoother through short transitional pieces or effective mood setters, such as choral calls to prayer or baptisms.

- Discuss ways to improve the continuity of the service through careful, cohesive worship planning.

Mission or outreach chairs:
- Ask about special mission projects for the year, e.g., an annual mission fair—and if you could be helpful in some way. Could you provide a choir, creating a festive atmosphere and perhaps drawing a larger audience?
- If there is a particular Sunday with a mission emphasis, suggest you jointly plan special music.
- Ask if they would be interested in cosponsoring a children's or youth choir trip to sing for retirement homes, hospitals, or hospices.

Church secretarial staff:
- Let them know how much you appreciate all they do for the church and the staff, particularly in the positive way they engage the people of the church on a daily basis.
- Ask if there are any ways that you could make their work easier or more effective.
- Tell them how much you would appreciate it if they would talk up the choir program whenever that opportunity presents itself. Ask to be contacted if families or individuals express an interest in singing.

Leaders of the church-sponsored scouting troops:
- Ask if they ever sing at their meetings and if they would occasionally like some help leading the songs? By getting to know the scout troop and making yourself available occasionally in their meetings, you may eventually recruit a few members for your youth choir.
- If you share responsibility for developing ideas for special worship events, help set up a Sunday each year when the scouts can be recognized in worship, serving as ushers, perhaps reading the Scriptures, and so on.

Choral and instrumental directors in nearby high schools:
- Make an appointment to introduce yourself to these colleagues. Say that since you are both teaching music to youth, you would be pleased to be of service in some way helpful, e.g., running a few sectionals as your time permits.
- Ask if you might compare your lists of choir members to determine if there are experienced singers in one choir but not the other. Also try to get a list from the band and orchestra, which is where the best musicians are.
- Ask for the dates of their concerts and try to attend them.
- Ask if they would be interested in presenting a choral or instrumental concert in your church as a "dress rehearsal" for a concert at the school, a contest, or a tour.

CHAPTER 34

STIMULATING CURIOSITY

Once you have thought through what is important about the choir program and have begun using those goals to build your support system, it is time to make the choirs the "talk of the halls." You want people to notice the new sense of energy, and hear about the special plans for each choir in the year ahead. Take every opportunity to put the idea of singing in a choir in the public's eye. The more people see and hear about choir, the more it becomes a topic of conversation. That leads inevitably to more people considering singing themselves or encouraging their family members and friends who ought to be singing. Finding ways to stimulate curiosity about the choir program opens the doors to having hundreds of people recruiting for you.

Here are some useful ideas for creating a buzz within the institution and community about your music program.

GENERAL RECRUITING TIPS

- Publicize "carrots" for each ensemble. Every choir director who hopes to attract new members to a choir needs a "carrot to dangle in front of the horse." The carrot proven most effective as an enticement in youth choir recruiting is some type of trip. It doesn't especially matter where or when, but if it means an overnight or two away from home with their friends, choir members want to be there. They don't like the idea of being left at home. Other carrots might include the choir making a guest appearance at some special event, performances with guest instrumentalists, or a variety of service projects.

- Remind your current singers that *they* are the key to recruiting success! In preparation for the most significant concert or service at the end of every season, print on the back of the programs, or on an insert, quotes from current singers in which they describe what they most like about choir. Take the time in a rehearsal for every member to write two or three sentences. Make it clear to your choir members that these quotes should be enticing and exciting enough to draw others into the choir. The object is that those reading the quotes will wish they were in choir, and therefore seriously consider signing up next year. Each quote needs to be accompanied by a name and grade. Once you have all the quotes in hand, choose the most intriguing twelve or so—whatever fits well on the page. There is no more effective recruiting tool. For a new choir, go to the director of a well-established choir and get quotes from those singers, so that your potential choir members can see how much fun singing in a choir could be. Here are some sample quotes from my own youth choir members:

—*Singing in choir is like making a pizza. Sure, it takes a while to grate the cheese, make the sauce, and roll the dough, but the final product is so worth it!*

—*In the middle of a week packed with tests and classes, choir is a great break with your friends.*

—*There is a bond among choir members—it's like any other team.*

—*Singing is one of the few activities you can do for a lifetime, and choir is a great way to get started.*

—*Choir is a terrific experience for freshmen, because you meet new people and make lasting friendships.*

—*Not only is the sound superior, but also there is such a spirit of enthusiasm, friendship, and enjoyment of music. Joining choir was one of the best decisions I ever made!*

—*The director is energetic and every rehearsal is fun.*

—*There is nothing as rewarding as knowing the chorus sounds wonderful, and you helped make that happen.*

—*The choir lets you form great friendships that otherwise probably wouldn't exist.*

• Have students place recruiting information cards under windshield wipers of the cars in the parking lot. These card-sized advertisements need to be attractive and enticing, making singing in choirs of all ages sound like too much fun to pass up. For churches, the best time is Easter morning, recruiting for the next year. For schools, the best time is about a week before information about course selection for the next year is sent home. This is an effective tool for making choir the "talk of the town" in advance of the time to sign up for the next season.

- Take advantage of every publication that goes out from the institution to create excitement about the choirs, to urge potential singers of all ages to consider seriously how much they might enjoy singing, and to state how much you would like to see them involved. For those with even the slightest interest, ask them to give you a call or send you an e-mail for more details (be sure to include your phone number and e-mail address).
- Design your own eye-catching "espionage cards" for gathering the names of potential singers. For churches, these cards in the pews may say, "Psst . . . If the person sitting next to you has a nice voice, write his or her name on this card and slip it into the offering plate!" For schools, hand out recruiting cards to every possible student organization or related class that say, "If you know of someone who would make a good choir member, put his or her name on this card and return it to (put your name) or leave it for me at the front desk."
- For the three weeks preceding the first rehearsal (for churches) or course-selection time (for schools), fill the hallways with a variety of choir recruiting posters that promote singing as a lot of fun.
- Using digital photography technology, prepare and share a post-trip DVD with background music and trip photographs.

ADDITIONAL RECRUITING TIPS FOR CHURCHES

- Give minitalks to all Sunday school divisions (all ages) and church social and service organizations. Select an appropriate approach for the age group you are addressing:

  —With the adults, emphasize the therapeutic benefits of singing, including the chance to step away from the other pressures of life one evening each week. At the same time, aiming at parents and grandparents, go through the "Why Bother" list of potential philosophical benefits for their children and grandchildren who participate in the choirs. Urge them to be proactive in giving this lifelong gift of music to their children or grandchildren.

  —With the youth, talk about how much fun choir is going to be, play twenty seconds of an enticing recording of a good youth choir, and talk about special performances and other choir events, e.g., community service activities, choir dinners, parties, or weekend trips.

—With children, speak slower and more gently but still tell them enthusiastically (remember your "default" joy from chapter 16) about some special activity for their choir coming up in the year ahead. For the children's choir, this may take the form of an annual musical or a field trip to sing at a retirement home. If you take this type of field trip, have your adult chaperones take along several digital cameras. When the short musical program by your children's choir is finished, have the children gather for photos around each of the audience members, sending the photos to the retirees for wonderful memories of the children's visit.

• Using digital photography technology, prepare a visual recording of choir highlights of the year (special performances, projects, parties, candid shots, and trips) on a DVD with background music of the choir singing.

CHAPTER 35

THE "HIT LIST": GATHERING NAMES TO GO AFTER

FINDING THE NAMES OF POTENTIAL CHOIR MEMBERS

- Take a moment in a rehearsal to have current choir members fill out index cards with the names of adults, youth, or families with children who might be potential choir members (don't limit that list to church members). After adding the names to your own master recruiting list, have your choir members take the cards home with them and call those prospects during the week. The purpose of the calls is to tell these choir prospects a little about the choir: how enjoyable it is, how friendly the members are, what a thrill people get from singing, and how much it would mean if they would consider singing in the choir. At the next rehearsal, your callers should give you the results, plus any added information such as home address, e-mail address, cell phone number, etc. This process should be repeated each September and January.
- Go over the current student directory with music teachers who taught most of your current students in the past, asking them to highlight the stronger musicians and leaders.
- Check old choir lists for supposedly temporary dropouts who then never returned; for youth and children, remember that the lists you need to check are of the lower grade levels.
- Offer one-time free voice lessons to anyone who would like to be able to sing better, no strings attached. Once a person experiences the joy of singing, they almost always end up joining a choir.

SPECIFIC IDEAS FOR CHURCHES

- Ask your minister to preach a sermon in late August or early September on the stewardship of our talents, using our talents in support of the church. As a part of the sermon, have the congregation fill out a talent survey checklist of their personal skills, experience, and special interests. Make sure that the checklist includes both choral and instrumentalist experience and the ability to read music. You can uncover some exceptional talent hidden away in the pews.
- After the service, have a well-advertised open house in the choir room with coffee, punch, and delicious things to eat provided by the various choirs (or by the parents of the younger choirs). The room should be enticingly set up for a wonderful rehearsal, well organized and bright, with lovely choral music being played. Current choir members of various ages serve as hosts, identified by a button that reads ASK ME ABOUT THE CHOIRS. Post a blank list in a prime location with a heading "Tell Us about Others Who Would Make Good Choir Members." Information and registration sheets should be available. It is vital that you get contact information about anyone who shows any interest in singing before they get away. So often people need that extra nudge to join, but if you have no way of contacting them, you might lose those prospects.
- Ask for five minutes during every new-members class or orientation to talk about the choir program and what it has to offer to every member of their families. For the adults, emphasize the angle of service to the church. Reassure them that even if they haven't sung in a choir before, if they enjoy music and can carry a tune, you can teach them everything else they need to know. Regarding choirs for their children, mention the lifelong joy of music they could open up for their children. Being in a choir for any age is a good way to make new friends quickly in a new church. As the new members introduce themselves, listen to their speaking voices and then be proactive with those that seem as if they would have a nice singing voice.
- If new members are asked to complete a questionnaire, make sure there is a place on the form to indicate their experience in music, e.g., have they ever played an instrument or sung in a choir; can they read music? Be certain this information gets to you right away, and then move quickly to invite their participation in the music program.
- Get to know the school choral and instrumental directors in your area. Sit in on a few rehearsals and casually meet some of the youth (or children). Let the directors know that you

are willing to help run sectionals or assist in any way if they could ever use the help. Ask to see old programs, noting any youth or children involved in the school music programs that might be enticed into joining your church choirs. Then have you own youth (or children) make the recruiting contacts.

SPECIFIC IDEAS FOR SCHOOLS

- Develop a short questionnaire asking students about their musical abilities and experiences (instrumental, vocal, and music reading ability and so on). Give a set to each advisor or homeroom teacher, inquiring whether they would be willing to have their students fill them out and then return the results to you. After compiling the information, send a letter in a personalized envelope to each student with strong interest or experience in music, saying how pleased you are to know of his or her interest. Follow up the letter with a personal phone call.
- Ask to be given five minutes to speak to new students when they come on campus for testing or orientation. In your presentation to the students, give them some of the exciting highlights of the year ahead. Play a short excerpt from the best of last year's choir performances. Tell these new students that you would love to have them consider being a part of the choir—emphasize that singing in choir is a great way to make a lot of new friends quickly and to feel they are really a part of their new school.
- Talk to private teachers (instrumental and vocal) who work with students from the school. Tell them that you will be urging as many of your students as possible to sign up for private lessons. In return, ask if they would speak positively to their students about singing in choir. Especially try to get as many instrumentalists as possible into the choir. They are often the ones with the musical background that is such an asset to sight-reading.

PUBLISHING A MOST-WANTED RECRUITING "HIT LIST"

- Using the names gathered through the various means listed earlier, publish a "Most-Wanted Choir Members" hit list. Display the list in several different places in the institution and in several different media, e.g., newsletters, e-mail, bulletin announcements, website. Add to the list a request that persons reading it should call those on the list whom they know and urge them to join the choir. If a conflict keeps individuals from joining choir, ask when that obligation will be over and whether you may call again then. Immediately put that name in a *tickler file* (a business term for a dated file of future responsibilities). When that date arrives, call each person and reissue the invitation. If they come up with additional conflicts, go through the process again . . . *but never quit going after them.*

CHAPTER 36

RECRUITING STRATEGIES FOR YOUTH (GRADES 7–12)

ENTICING THE LEADERS

- Find and court the leaders. Ask around about who the movers and shakers are among the youth. Who are the ones who seem to give direction to the group? Don't ignore the troublemakers; they often have more natural leadership skills than anyone else. All they need is better direction and some affirmation for the good they could do.
- Invite these key youth out as a group for hamburgers on you. Tell them that, when you asked who the leaders are among the youth, *their* names rose to the top. (Affirmations like this give a positive sense of self-worth, something most youth don't experience often enough.) Tell them about your ideas for an upbeat, fun, and quality youth choir. Let them see that you care about them and that you would be a fun director.
- Tell them that you are working hard to develop something special for the students, but that you need their help to pull it off. They know the other youth, and those youth look to them for leadership. Explain that most of the youth here don't know you yet and might be hesitant to give choir a chance, unless leaders like them put out the word and help get this thing off the ground. This is an opportunity to use their considerable leadership skills to do immense good. Would they be willing to be part of your recruiting team?
- Ask them to come up with a few more names of vibrant, upbeat youth who could help out with a recruiting "phone-calling brigade" and party. Tell them you need a few youth from each grade level who are not shy and who love a challenge.

THE PHONE-CALLING BRIGADE

- Find a weekend or early evening when several of the offices in your church or school are not being used and get permission to use those phones for a couple of hours. Then put together a "calling brigade" of your handpicked leaders and other youth they suggested. Provide free pizza and a quick training session on what to say.
- Have a fake phone at the training session and actually demonstrate how to speak enthusiastically by role-playing with various youth being the callers and others being the callees.
- Remind your callers about the importance of this "phone-calling brigade" in developing a wonderful choir. Also remind them that they were chosen because of their leadership.
- Show your callers how to get started with the conversation, introducing themselves and then immediately saying something like, "There is something exciting going on that some of us think you should know about."
- Explain the "Phone-Calling Brigade Information Sheet" (see below).
- Have the name of each potential youth singer (gathered in the previous weeks) on separate index cards with as much information as you have available, e.g., phone number, grade, school, previous musical experience if known, major interests if known. On the back of each card have duplicated the following, which needs to be filled out during each call:

    ＿＿ Would definitely be interested in choir
    ＿＿ Might be interested . . . maybe
    ＿＿ Absolutely no interest

- Spread the cards out on a table and allow your callers to choose cards of youth they would like to call. Then, keeping in mind grade levels, split the remaining cards among all the callers.
- Set a reasonable time limit—no more than two hours of calling.
- Urge your callers to sell hard, making it nearly impossible for those to whom they talk to say no. Callers should talk fast and keep talking, so that there isn't the opportunity for callees to turn callers down until they have given their entire pitch!
- Make the process a fun contest for your callers by offering free movie passes to the person or team (pairing in twos is often a good idea) who sign up the most new members. Once the choir is meeting regularly, you can also offer movie

tickets or even a gift certificate of some kind to the person who brings the most new members in a three-week period. Supportive adults in the church are usually glad to pick up the tab.

- Many of the youth called will respond that they don't know how to sing. The callers must convince the prospects that the director can teach whatever they need to know . . . and that they *never* ever have to sing by themselves.
- If the response is even slightly positive, ask if they have interested friends whom they could invite to bring along. Many prospective members who wouldn't have the courage to come to choir alone will come with a friend, if you give them that idea.
- After the call, the caller must check off the appropriate response on the back of each card and jot down any additional information that might be helpful to the director in following up.
- If no one is home, leave the whole presentation on the message machine, even if you have to call back twice to fit it in. Ask them to give you a call back when they can, and that, if you don't hear from them, you or the director will be back in touch.
- Make sure you get back all cards before the callers leave.

PHONE-CALLING BRIGADE INFORMATION SHEET

Develop an informational sheet for callers to use while doing their recruiting, which could include information such as the following:

- Details of an upcoming out-of-town trip with at least one overnight; tell the prospective choir members how great it would be to have them on that trip, having a good time with the group.
- The types of music you will be singing, emphasizing the livelier, upbeat styles for recruiting purposes.
- Choir is a terrific way to make new friends.
- Choir can be a significant college hook, because when listed on a college application, choir participation shows balance in life choices and a sense of culture and sophistication; choir is one way in which you may be of value to a college.
- Singing is therapeutic, a nice break from the pressures of studying and sports.
- Say something nice about the director (the callers decide on their own what to say here, but it is important that they leave an impression that the director will be fun to work with).

- Details of when and where the choir rehearses and how often it performs.
- End with "What about it . . . how about giving choir a shot?"

FOLLOWING UP

- Separate the calling cards into three stacks according to the responses to the questions on the back.
- Those that answered "definitely interested" should get a short personal welcome letter from you right away, reminding them when and where the first rehearsal will be and saying you look forward to seeing them there.
- Those that answered "maybe" get a personal call the next day from you.
- Those that answered "absolutely not" are sent an immediate letter saying that you are sorry they aren't able to work out choir this year, but you hope they will keep it in mind for the future. Also tell them that you'll be checking with them again next year.

CHAPTER 37

A RECRUITING CREDO

There is no doubt in my mind that if you develop your determined-to-succeed attitude and then use these recruiting ideas fully, you will end up with a full choir long before you expect it.

Here are some final thoughts, some "Kempisms," to keep you safely on the path to successful choir recruiting.

- Recruiting is not something you do once in a while in an emergency, but rather a new way of life.

- Remember that enthusiasm is contagious; let yours be obvious and continuous. The power of a smile is incredibly effective.

- Make *unstoppable determination* your overriding default attitude; check yours out constantly.

What are you waiting for—a miracle? You have to make our own miracles, and you will by following these procedures. Take one step at a time, and your miracles will walk in that rehearsal room door!

POSTLUDE

WHERE HAS ALL THE BEAUTY GONE?

Where has all the beauty gone? News broadcasts portray murders and mayhem, wars and shamed leaders. Sports often emphasize violence and winning at all costs. Advertisers stimulate our desires for instant gratification. Into that often-callous world we choir directors help bring the timeless beauty of music. A choir may serve as an example of what a caring community should be, with directors and singers combining their individual talents to accomplish something more significant than any of us could accomplish alone. Choir members listen to one another's parts and learn how to go forward together, giving the priority back and forth as they share the melodies. Then they take the fruits of that labor and share it with audiences, multiplying the positive effect countless times.

Wouldn't it be wonderful if the world were like that? We spread our musical wings to fly and along the way offer to take audiences with us. We have made our choice. Rather than be discouraged by another news broadcast, we directors and our singers have chosen to be a part of the soothing and uplifting effect of music. The world needs our contributions to what is novel and good about life. It is my hope that the solutions offered in *The Choral Challenge* will help you and your choirs make ever more beautiful music.

—*Michael Kemp*

ACKNOWLEDGMENTS

Writing *The Choral Challenge* was a significant undertaking requiring the ongoing support and encouragement of mentors, friends, professional colleagues, and family. I owe a debt of gratitude to them all.

Germantown Academy made the initial writing possible through several generous Kast Grants for summer writing. The Academy was also integral to the eventual completion of the book by awarding me a leave of absence from my teaching responsibilities in order to take advantage of an artist colony residency. I am especially grateful to James Connor, Head of School; Suzanne Perot, Assistant Head of School; and John Ball, Head of the Upper School. The Ragdale Foundation, the aforementioned artist colony, provided me with six weeks of unparalleled serenity and inspiration, a marvelous incubator for reflection and disciplined writing.

This being my first writing project of this scope, I relied heavily on an array of exceptional proofreaders. Janet Easlea has a wonderful eye for detail, and her unremitting zeal for this project was a great source of inspiration. Barbara Keaton is an exceptional teacher who guided me toward clarity and accessibility in what I had to say. David Leshan, retired Head of the English Department of Germantown Academy, taught me much about becoming a better writer and made many valuable suggestions. Dr. Bradford Davis, besides adding medical expertise to the chapters on the voice, continually broadened my thinking with the depth of his perception. Janice Kemp was an exemplary proofreader whose keen attention to detail and infallible instincts were extraordinarily effective. Timothy Evers, a conductor early in his career, read with a particular eye toward relevancy and practical results, testing out many of the book's procedures and concepts on his own choirs. He was also, along with Steven Herman of Germantown Academy, my computer and music notation technical expert, sometimes working straight through the night via cell phone from his office to the artist colony. I also want to express my deepest thanks to my mother, Helen Kemp, for reading my manuscripts so thoughtfully, for keeping ever before me the aspect of being of service to others, and for sharing with me the insights of her almost seventy years of working with choirs.

I am particularly indebted to the professionals who shared their unique expertise with me. Julia Kemp and her husband, Guy Rothfuss, twenty-five-year veterans of successful opera singing throughout Europe, were invaluable with their insights about the voice. Renowned vocal authority and Professor of Otolaryngology Dr. Robert Sataloff, his singing-voice specialist Margaret Baroody, and his speech therapist Michelle Horman brought me to a completely new understanding of how the voice works. Judith Grodowitz, one of the finest teachers of the Alexander Technique in the country, renewed my whole concept of posture and alignment.

But the day-to-day work of bringing this book to fruition was much the meticulous and patient work of my GIA editor, Neil Borgstrom. A church musician himself, Neil believed from the first in the value of book, reading each word with a striking attention to detail. His perceptive questions about the intentions of sentences suffused the book with unambiguous clarity, usefulness, and accessibility. For all his careful work and relentless commitment to excellence, this book is partly his.

APPENDIX A

Pitch Designations

Pitch Designations of the U.S.A. Standards Association

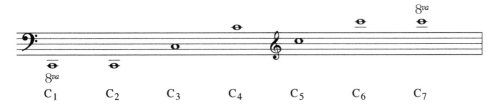

C_1 C_2 C_3 C_4 C_5 C_6 C_7

APPENDIX B

IPA COMMON DESIGNATIONS

e - say

æ - cat

ɑ - father

ɔ - saw

i - see

ɛ - bed, Italian "eh"

ɪ - sit

o - so

ɔɪ - joy

u - soon

ŋ - hang

For more designations of the International Phonetics Alphabet, see the appendixes of Richard Miller, *Solutions for Singers: Tools for Performers and Teachers* (New York: Oxford University Press, 2004).

SELECTED BIBLIOGRAPHY

Alsobrook, Joseph. *Pathways: A Guide for Energizing & Enriching Band, Orchestra, & Choral Programs*. Chicago: GIA Publications, 2002.

Bennis, Warren. *Reinventing Leadership: Strategies to Empower the Organization*. New York: Simon and Schuster Audio, 1996.

Brown, Les. *The Courage to Live Your Dreams*. HarperAudio, 1991.

Cameron, Julia. *The Artist's Way: A Spiritual Path to Higher Creativity*. New York: Putnam (Penguin Putnam), 1992, 2002.

Carnegie, Dale. *How to Win Friends and Influence People*. New York: Simon and Schuster, 1936.

Chandler, Steve. *100 Ways to Motivate Yourself: Change Your Life Forever*. Franklin Lakes, NJ: Career Press, 2001.

Crow, Robin. *Jump and the Net Will Appear: Discovering the Art of Achievement and the Rhythm of Success*. Novato, CA: New World Library, 2002.

Decker, Harold, and Julius Herford. *Choral Conducting: A Symposium*. New York: Meredith Corporation, 1973.

Grun, Bernard. *The Timetables of History: A Horizontal Linkage of People and Events*. Rev. ed. New York: Simon and Schuster, 1991.

Hill, Napoleon. Keys to Success: *The 17 Principles of Personal Achievement*. Audio Renaissance Tapes, 1994.

Hines, Jerome. *The Four Voices of Man*. New York: Limelight Editions, 1997.

McGinnis, Alan Loy. *Bringing the Best Out of People: How to Excel in Helping Others Excel*. Minneapolis: Augsburg Publishing, 1985.

Miller, Richard. *Solutions for Singers: Tools for Performers and Teachers*. New York: Oxford University Press, 2004.

Noble, Weston. *Creating the Special World*. Chicago: GIA Publications, 2005.

Peck, M. Scott. *Further Along the Road Less Traveled*. New York: Simon and Schuster, 1993.

Sandys, Celia. *We Shall Not Fail: The Inspiring Leadership of Winston Churchill*. New York: Portfolio (Penguin Group), 2003.

Sanders, Tim. *The Likability Factor*. New York: Crown Publishers, 2005.

Sataloff, Robert Thayer. *Vocal Health and Pedagogy*. San Diego: Singular Publishing Group, 1998.

Sataloff, Robert Thayer, and Brenda Smith. *Choral Pedagogy*. San Diego: Singular Publishing Group, 2000.

See, Carolyn. *Making a Literary Life: Advise for Writers and Other Dreamers*. New York: Random House, 2002.

Shepherd, Margaret. *The Art of the Handwritten Note*. New York: Broadway Books (Random House), 2002.

Tharp, Twyla. *The Creative Habit: Learn It and Use It for Life*. New York: Simon and Schuster, 2003.

Winston, Stephanie. *Getting Organized*. New York: Warner Books, 1978.

INDEX

Page numbers of key words within Troubleshooting Common Vocal Problems (4–45) or Warm-up Exercises (108–165) are in **bold**. These sections are not generally otherwise indexed.